Start Loving Again

How to Resolve All Trust Issues, Build Trust in Relationship and Create a Loving Relationship You Deserve

Ellie K. Flores

Seven Suns Book Press

© Copyright 2022 by Ellie K. Flores - All rights reserved.

The content contained within this book may not be reproduced, duplicated or transmitted without direct written permission from the author or the publisher.

Under no circumstances will any blame or legal responsibility be held against the publisher, or author, for any damages, reparation, or monetary loss due to the information contained within this book, either directly or indirectly.

Legal Notice:

This book is copyright protected. It is only for personal use. You cannot amend, distribute, sell, use, quote or paraphrase any part, or the content within this book, without the consent of the author or publisher.

Disclaimer Notice:

Please note the information contained within this document is for educational and entertainment purposes only. All effort has been executed to present accurate, up to date, reliable, complete information. No warranties of any kind are declared or implied. Readers acknowledge that the author is not engaged in the rendering of legal, financial, medical or professional advice. The content within this book has been derived from various sources. Please consult a licensed professional before attempting any techniques outlined in this book.

By reading this document, the reader agrees that under no circumstances is the author responsible for any losses, direct or indirect, that are incurred as a result of the use of the information contained within this document, including, but not limited to, errors, omissions, or inaccuracies.

Contents

1. Introduction — 1
2. Trust Issues In The Relationship — 7
3. Is He Too Controlling? — 12
4. I Did Nothing Wrong, Why Is He Jealous? — 21
5. He Wants To Stay In Contact 24/7 — 32
6. He Keeps Checking My Phone And Asking Where I Am — 41
7. He Thinks I Will Leave Him For Another Man — 50
8. He Keeps Lying To Me — 57
9. He Cheated...This Is The End! — 66
10. What Happens Next? — 79
11. Is The Relationship Salvageable? — 83
12. Am I Being Stupid Or Smart? — 88

13. But I Am Still Hurt And Angry	92
14. The Preventive Measures Checklist	98
15. Putting In The Work From The Get-Go	100
16. Actions That Violate Trust	102
17. Traits That Make You Appear Untrustworthy	106
18. Being Honest, Transparent, And Open To Dialogues	109
19. Let's Fall In Love Again	114
20. Conclusion	124
Also By	128
Author Note	129

Introduction

IT ALL BEGAN WITH a ping in the middle of the night. Who could be texting him this late? Why did he have to leave the room to reply? What is taking him so long? The bitter and dizzy feelings of suspicion were grounded in my mind. Suddenly, everything started to make sense. Why had he started spending more time at the gym? Why was he always on the phone? Why was he cautious about what he wore, and whether his socks matched or not? The awful confirmation of my suspicions made me so angry that I started to shake. I was glad he wasn't around because I had some thinking to do.

Trust may be hard to define, but you know when it's lost. When a partner ends up cheating or is caught telling a lie, you know it's gone out of the window. Suddenly, all the pastel colors in your beautiful world turn to greys and browns. You feel like you have just withdrawn the energy and investment you had in them. You go on an internal strike. You can't seem to show sympathy to them after being hurt or wronged. We pull away and no longer feel connected on the same level. Loss of trust is the cruelest of things.

If you had your heart broken because you caught your partner lying, cheating, or going behind your back, it can feel like the end of the world. You must be questioning their every intention because nothing seems real anymore. You feel like you had your eyes shut or behind a mask and suddenly it has come off and made you see the ugly side of your partner. It can be heartbreaking. You might just want to walk away or run off to a different continent, but deep down, know that there is still some mending that you can do.

Relationships are like oceans. Some days, they are calm and let the boater enjoy the calmness of the waves and the bright sun, and some days, the wildest of waves crash against the turf, rocking your inner core, hoping for the winds to calm down and let the sun restore the peace. Some days, looking at the horizon, you seem like it will never end and then on some days, you are tested for not knowing your way and following in the currents blinding. There are days where you have to struggle to stay afloat when the lifeboat tumbles over and other days, you can bask in all the sunshine graciously pouring down, warming you with love.

Relationships, whether new or old, take time, commitment, compassion, and trust.

Trust in a relationship is the glue that holds it together. It helps partners connect on a deeper level. It binds them in a knot of love and compassion for one another. When you trust someone, it means that you trust their judgment, intention, and affection. You have faith in their companionship. You believe that they can do you no wrong. It is like expecting someone close. You choose to rely on their word, action, and behavior because deep down, you know that they will have your back, love you for who you are, and take a bullet for you.

Different people have different interpretations of the term "trust." Some believe it is about feeling comfortable in opening up with someone and letting them see your vulnerable side. Some think it has more to do with being transparent and open. Some say it is about having faith in your partner that they can never have any ill intentions towards you. Some say it is about reassurance that no matter what, together two people can face any battles, arguments, or fights. Some see it as a means to heal from a misunderstanding. Some argue it is what makes one feel secure. Some believe when a partner says they trust them, it means they are their priority in life. And then, some people think having trust is about giving each other some space to breathe and do their own thing.

Whichever definitions seem the best to you, let's all agree that it is the foundation of every interpersonal relationship you have. Trust is the essence of love. It makes you want to believe in someone when they say they will love you and be loyal to you forever. It makes you want to rely on them and feel comfortable confiding in them your darkest secrets. You know they will keep them safe.

It makes you want to be loved and part of something bigger than yourself. When you trust someone, you share a common goal, purpose, and willingness to count on one another. You willingly do your part and make the efforts the relationship requires to stay strong. You don't just offer your presence but also your dedication, energy, talent, and thoughts on what works and what doesn't.

In simpler terms, trust defines confidence in the integrity of a loved one. It goes hand in hand with reliability. When you trust someone, you feel safe with them emotionally and physically. You know you can depend on them. But when it's broken, all hell breaks loose.

So how can you mend things? How can you go back to trusting your partner? How can you prevent yourself from breaking your partner's trust initially? How can you heal and fall in love with them again?

These are valid questions that demand our attention, perspective, and time.

Together, let's look at these various concerns partners have when they are in a relationship, no matter what phase they are in. Starting with the most common trust issues and how they affect you and your partner, we dive right into what can be done once the trust has been broken. It is also for those who have just started a new relationship and worry that their experience at love will ruin the beautiful thing they have. They are worried that their possessiveness and insecurities will make their partner want to break up with them.

Most of the time, we are unable to identify the root causes of a lack of trust. We don't know who to blame or what caused it. The objective of the book is to help you establish trust in your relationship, regain it if it has been lost, and prevent you from losing it again. Together, we shall explore through the lives of many people and their stories about the trust issues they faced in their relationships and what advice we can offer them. In the end, there are some fun and exciting exercises for couples to try out and learn more about the kind of relationship they have, as well as how much work it needs.

The practical tips and advice come backed by science and professional marriage counselors and relationship coaches who seem to have figured out what keeps relationships sailing smoothly.

Part One

TRUST ISSUES IN THE RELATIONSHIP

RECENT SCIENTIFIC EVIDENCE SUGGESTS that we are hardwired to trust others. Our brains crave the connection and feeling of devotion that comes from trusting someone. Perhaps this is why betrayal feels so real and painful. It's a wake-up call for the brain to stop dreaming about the perfectness of things and see reality for what it is. When trust is broken, there is a short-circuit in neurobiology, making it difficult to fall into the same trap again. In the study, researchers wanted to shed light on what drives us to trust one another, especially during a time of potential risk.

For the study, participants were under the illusion that they were playing a game with three different players: a stranger, a close friend, and a computerized slot machine. In reality, the participants were playing against a computer with a simple algorithm that reciprocated actions worthy of trust systematically 50% of the time.

Based on the perception of trust, participants reported positive interactions with a close friend as more rewarding than when they were interacting with the computerized slot machine or a stranger. The game's theme revolved around economic investment. All the participants seemed more eager to invest with a close friend. This illustrated our innate desire to seek connection and form close-knit bonds with whomever we can, even when the trust was based on Ponzi schemes as such.

Researchers studied the brain imaging of the participants throughout the game and found two regions actively engaged when they thought they were playing with a close friend. They saw an increase in the activity of the medial prefrontal cortex and the ventral striatum. The activity correlated with positive social value because participants thought they were playing with a good friend.

The medial prefrontal cortex regulates how we perceive another person's mental state and what happens outside our current focus of attention. The same region also plays a crucial role in the retrieval and consolidation of memories as well as decision-making.

Together, these regions provide sufficient evidence that participants felt positive and comfortable when they played with a close friend. Interestingly, despite the reality of the situation, feelings of trust occurred. Participants continued to trust a close friend throughout the game.

This study illustrates the mechanisms fundamental for building trust and social value. The willingness to trust someone is in our DNA. This is one reason why working together as a team has improved the chances of survival for our species. Having faith that the other person means no harm and is a benefactor is an intrinsic property.

Having faith means trust. Trusting someone takes courage. It takes guts to open up to someone and let them become a part of your life. It takes strength to share with them everything that is yours, including your deepest darkest secrets, and hope that they will keep them safe. As trust binds relationships together, mistrust pulls them apart. Bit by bit, and then all of a sudden when you can no longer see them in the eyes because you know the love you had for them has vanished.

Mistrust plays a dominant role in an individual's life. Disappointments and betrayals are the roots of the issue. Mistrust is a genuine response to feeling abandoned or betrayed. Mistrust can result in anger, anxiety, and even self-doubt. While exploring the theme of trust, we must understand where trust issues stem from? What makes it difficult for one person to trust another, even when they haven't cheated, lied, or done anything remotely similar to deserve it?

The most common reason for trust issues is early experiences and interactions. Several aversive experiences can contribute to a child's mistrust and lack of confidence. For instance, inconsistent responses from parents and failing to deliver on their promises make a child insecure. An unexpected outburst from a parent in rage shatters their trust in the predictability of the world. Being physically or sexually abused as a child can also trigger dissociative states in young ones.

Traumatic life events can also lead to trust issues in adults. For example, illnesses, accidents, loss of a loved one, being robbed, being cheated on, or left for another person. Being physically violated or attacked can also lead to a lack of trust in others. This happens when instances like assault or rape occurred. Men and women in the military have also shown difficulty in trust because of the wartime violence they have been exposed to. They exhibit signs of post-traumatic stress disorder (PTSD) and perceive everything and everyone as dangerous. Anxiety is often common with this type of trauma. Veterans suffering from PTSD go to great lengths to feel safe and establish feelings of security. In many cases, they isolate themselves and avoid relying on others emotionally or physically.

This is why they may have trouble trusting their partners or become trustworthy partners themselves. Due to the kind of exposure they have had during the time when they were in service, they are unable to trust their partner completely or lose trust in them often.

When partners aren't fully honest and transparent or send missed messages to the other, it can create an atmosphere of not only confusion but also alienation. Confusion can lead to the breakdown of mutual trust among partners. Partners become afraid of intimacy and over-dependence on their partners. They emotionally shut down or avoid spending time together. When questioned, they fail to provide valid reasons for the lack of closeness, which further elevates the issue.

So how can we overcome the most common issues in relationships? How can we learn to be more communicative and open with our partners? How can we ensure that the relationship stays solid and unbreakable?

It calls for an evaluation and discussion of the most common trust issues men and women complain of, whether they have just started dating their partner or have been with them for long. Starting from the very obvious and most common trust issues among partners, and couples is anxiety about a relationship that leads to overbearing control of the other.

Is He Too Controlling?

JOSHUA AND KATHERINE HAVE been together for over three months now. They met on a casual date set by their mutual friends and instantly clicked. Joshua thought Katherine was the most humble of beings with a heart of gold. She worked as a pro bono lawyer in a small firm in Brooklyn. Her work kept her busy most of the days. Even when she was home, she was getting calls from all parts of the city, wanting her to take their case. She loved every bit of her job.

In the beginning, Joshua appreciated that she was a dedicated woman. But lately, it had started to piss him off. She would reply late, not take his calls, and postpone plans.

Katherine, on the other hand, had been tired to the bone. The last month had been a rollercoaster ride with multiple cases. All she wanted was to come home to someone who understood what she did and didn't complain. She tried her best to stay in touch with Joshua but she couldn't be at his back and forth 24/7. Recently, his demands to meet and spend time together had increased. He had become impatient and rude. He would call her *a hundred times during work hours and leave messages back to back. If she didn't pick up, he would come to the office and fight about it. She just wanted him to understand. Even today, he had called a gazillion times, asking where she was and what she was doing. She just wanted to spend some time with a few friends visiting her from outside town and he couldn't even respect that. Why was he becoming this control freak? Why could he not understand that she too, had a life, apart from him? She never thought being in a relationship was this much work. She never anticipated that she would have to be policed about where she was and who she was with, every time she went out. She didn't know that she would have to beg for some space from her partner so that she can be herself. She was done fighting about it every other night. He didn't seem to care. He just wanted her to be with him every minute of the day, doing what he wanted to do.*

While everyone enjoys having control of their lives, controlling people enjoy having a say in other people's lives too. They want to control every aspect of other people's lives, crossing the line from being possessive to creepy.

Most of the time, when we hear the term "controlling partner," the image of someone that openly berates everyone in their path, constantly gives ultimatums or makes overt threats, comes to mind. We picture someone who loves to bully, is aggressive, and belittles every server they encounter or demands that their partner dress according to their liking from head to toe. Surely, those signs are troubling, to say the least; many show up quite differently.

Some controlling partners act out of a sense of heightened vulnerability and emotional fragility. They use a whole arsenal of tools to try to dominate their partners, whether they or their partners realize it or not. Some just go with the flow, thinking their partner is a romantic and wants to be invested in their lives. But this emotional manipulation is sneaky. Sometimes, it takes years for one to realize that they have been wronged all their lives. Manipulative controllers are experts at making the other partner feel guilty and play the villain. They know how to shame and know how to make their partner think that they are lucky enough to have someone as possessive and romantic as them. But this isn't a healthy situation and certainly not a healthy relationship.

Both partners should feel free to express and question. They should be able to enjoy their time together as well as apart. No one should have the power to guilt the other into doing something they want them to do.

Signs Your Partner Is Too Controlling

Since emotional manipulation can be deceiving, it is best to know if you are in a relationship with someone that is controlling and demanding. Below are some tell-tale signs that your partner is manipulative and controlling.

They Don't Accept Blame

More like, refuse to take responsibility for it at all. In the case of Joshua and Katherine, there is no talking to Joshua about giving her some space because she has tried it before and it didn't work. Joshua refuses to accept that what he demands is unacceptable. People like Joshua, who like to control their partners, are incapable of accepting their faults, even when his actions, like walking into her office for not taking his calls, are wrong. Instead, he has the guts to blame Katherine for not giving him time and making her feel guilty.

They Want To Be The Center Of Attention

This is rather obvious from the case that Joshua wants to be the only thing that should be on Katherine's mind 24/7. He wants to upstage her in every way he can. He wants to be in the limelight. He wants to be the center of attention at all times and that is another sign Katherine should look into.

They Can Be Unpredictable

There is no guessing what a controlling partner will do next. They might lose their cool, become aggressive, and begin to verbally abuse their partner. From telling you how great you look, they can swiftly transition into telling you that they are upset with you because you don't do as they say. The same is the case with Joshua who tries to control Katherine by wanting to know where she is and what she is doing all the time and if she fails to respond, he goes in to check for himself.

Score-Keeping

They will remind you of the one nice thing they did for you back then and then guilt-trip you by showing disappointment that you didn't do something special for them. They keep tabs on all the favors they did, even when they thought they did them out of love. Had you known they wanted something in return, you would have made them stop. For example, if they paid for dinner, or allowed you to stay at their place for one night, they will bring it up repeatedly, requesting similar favors in return. They may even go overboard with their generosity, just to keep you indebted to them.

They Isolate You From Your Friends And Family

Does your partner want you all for themselves? Do they often turn down offers from friends and families when they invite for dinner? Do they change plans of visiting them last minute without telling you? Do they make excuses like being sick or bribe you with weekend packages when you plan a get-together with your family? This is one of the most intrusive ways to control you. They control your movement. They want to know where you are all the time, who you are with, what plans you have for the weekend, are you meeting with your family members or not, etc. they are even interested in knowing about what you talked about with your sister or parent about on the phone the other day. Joshua did the same. Even though he knew Katherine was out with the friends, he kept bugging her with messages, wanting her to come home. Whether it's intimidation, threats, pouting, or blatant excuses, the plan is always to isolate you from your friends and family so that you don't have anyone else to rely on other than them.

They Lie

Truth is the bedrock of reality. Controlling partners want to control your reality. They will deny your reality by lying. They will lie about their behavior or yours. They will make sure that you know that you are the crazy one in the relationship and dare you to try to contradict them. They have a set of lies prepared to take you down as their backup. For example, if you demand some time away from them, they will tell you how you always want to get away from them and never want to be near. They will remind you of all those instances where you had told them to go, even casually. They will tell you how hurt they had been but never made you sense it. Clearly, it is a lie but someone that is in love, wouldn't see that.

They Gaslight You

When you demand an explanation for anything, they will tell you that you are being over-sensitive. If you bring up something they said to you last week, they would deny that they ever said it. Even if they do agree, they will tell you that you had it all wrong and they never intended to mean it. They will tell you that it's all in your head and they will be so sure of themselves that it will leave you second-guessing yourself.

They Hijack Conversations

Controlling partners use rhetorical questions, change the subject, correct constantly, and turn the tables around to get their point across. They don't give you any time to have a say. If you ask them something, they deflect the conversation by accusing you of something else. Their original point never gets addressed.

They Talk Excessively

Continuing from the same point, they don't encourage responses and being called out. They would talk excessively and combine different off-topics, leaving their partner unable to process their thoughts. Ultimately, they make their partner feel hostage and surrender.

If this is just the beginning of the relationship and you notice one or more of these signs already, make it very clear how you feel about the way they behave. They will, of course, be shocked at first because they don't believe they are control freaks, but letting it out means they have been warned. If their behavior remains the same, maybe it is time to rethink about getting serious.

What Can You Do About It

However, if you wish to stay and believe that something can be done to improve their behavior and feelings towards you, there are a few actionable steps that will help you get your word across. However, be prepared for a defensive power struggle because they aren't going to let go easily. But if you hold your ground and remain determined, they will have no choice but to give it. It won't happen overnight but eventually, they will stop trying to micromanage every aspect of your life.

First things first, as stated above, don't get into a power struggle with a controlling partner. They take it up as a challenge and are sure to bring their A-game. As they are experts at it, chances are they are going to beat you at it. So unless you want more yelling than getting your word across, we suggest you avoid getting in a one-on-one with them. They will look like high-powered layers, and destroy you with their excellent arguing skills. Their word-smithing will demolish your opinions or ideas. What you must do instead is use the "I feel..." approach. This is a tried and tested approach and comes recommended by many marriage counselors and relationship coaches. Ideally, you tell your partner how a certain behavior of theirs makes you feel. For example, suppose you want your partner to give you some space to be yourself. Start by appealing to their desire to control and tell them how their actions or possessiveness makes you feel rather than accusing them with, "You make me suffocated," say,

"I feel like I need to stop making you micromanage all my activities. I feel it is time to learn to do that on my own."

Notice how the two sentences evoke different emotions? In the first, it is raw and blatant, just out there. In the second, however, you make them feel proud of how good they are with their management and then suggest that you let them become a big girl and take care of yourself and your needs.

The second technique is to make them see how damaging and hurting their behavior is and how it affects your mental peace and the relationship. Again, this has to be done in a calm and relaxed manner, one where you don't come off as nagging or argumentative. You need to make them see your point by quoting very specific examples and their actions in them and then the outcome it led to. Be assertive but also polite in stating your terms. The terms are, of course, guidelines on how you wish to be treated instead. For example, suppose you are in an important meeting with a client and they keep texting and calling back, expecting to stay in touch. Instead of cutting the call or leaving their messages on seen, call back and state very clearly why you can't talk right now. Suggest another time, preferably in the next few hours so that they don't lose their calm. Also, express how you wish you could talk to them right now but your boss wouldn't let you. This would take away some of the blame from you and make them more considerate.

Finally, if they fail to listen and oblige with the terms and conditions you set, hate to be talked back, and emotionally manipulated, hold your ground, and set some sound boundaries and consequences. Let them know straight up that this type of behavior will not be tolerated and will only lead to more fights and conflicts between them. Stand your ground and see what they come up with in response. If they continue to stick to their old patterns, show them that you meant every word of what you said by requesting some space away from them so that they have some time to think about what they did. In the meantime, don't contact them unless they are sorry and want to improve.

I Did Nothing Wrong, Why Is He Jealous?

"ADAM, WE HAVE HAD this conversation a hundred times before too. He is my boss. I am not having an affair with him. We just talked for a while at the party. I can't ignore him if he comes up to speak to me. You were there. We talked about nothing but the project. His wife was there too. Did you not see how happy he looked in her company? Why do I have to keep explaining to you over and over again that nothing is going on between us? He is just friendly with everyone, that's all!"

The car ride back home from the party was like hell for Julianne. This wasn't the first time this topic had come up and caused a fight. Adam had this attitude towards every guy she met. Once Adam fought her because she gave directions to someone on the street. He was a foreigner and wanted to know which bus to take to get to a certain place. That had Adam all riled up and acting jealous. She remembered how happy she was to take him to this party only a few hours ago. It was the first time her company had allowed a plus one to be brought. But her excitement went down the drain when she noticed Adam being his usual self, *eyeing every other guy with suspicion. She didn't know what to make of his jealousy and whether she was going to endure the same behavior for long or not. Apart from that, Adam was a great, funny guy. He was the perfect partner but because of his jealous nature, Julianne was starting to rethink her decision to have said yes to his proposal.*

Is she in the wrong?

Jealousy, since the dawn of time, has been a prevalent emotion. In many films, art, and literature, this has remained a common and central theme. Shakespeare called it the green-eyed monster. We even have proof of it in the Biblical narrative. Remember the relationship between the two siblings Cain and Abel, sons of Adam? Remember how Cain sinned killing his brother in a fit of jealousy?

Jealousy in romantic relationships is similar. Although partners don't talk about it as openly, the emotion has been responsible for some of the biggest arguments and conflicts among partners. We feel jealous when we feel consumed with the pervading idea that we have weaknesses and limitations. We feel jealous when we lack things others have. The emotion is so strong that it takes away our attention from what we already have and becomes ungrateful towards it.

Some feel that a little jealousy in a relationship is natural and cute. It makes partners feel valued and important. When someone talks possessively about you, it makes you feel loved. And let's not forget, we have all felt a little jealous at some point in the relationship. We have felt possessive when at a restaurant, the waiter is being extra nice to our partner or someone at the bar sends them a free drink. We have felt jealous of our partners' female friends because they all seem so beautiful and fun. We feel jealous because we feel threatened by them and of the relationship they share. We feel like they would take away what is ours and worse, make them happier than we do. We feel replaceable and that isn't a good feeling at all. While most partners exhibit some jealousy occasionally, some depict it to a pathological degree. Their jealousy becomes so uncontrollable that it eats away the happiness there is, ultimately, leading to the end of the relationship.

Evolutionarily, philosophers and psychologists have long debated what jealousy is. Some believe that jealousy gives men and women a fitness advantage. Another research quotes that men are more prone to becoming jealous about their physical infidelity whereas women are more prone to becoming jealous about their emotional infidelity.

There are many factors or reasons why jealousy is so common among partners. The first factor that contributes to it is adapted from an evolutionary perspective. Two relevant theories explain the cause. The first theory is parental investment theory which explores that if we continue to take care of someone else's genes, we will feel jealous. For example, women are sure that they are the mother of their children. Men aren't always. Therefore, men show more symptoms of jealousy than females about their sexual infidelity. Since they can't have the same bond a mother has for the child, they feel jealous of the special bond. Women, on the other hand, are jealous about the emotional closeness with a competitor, such as another mother. They feel like they have to prove that they are the best of the lot and try to impress everyone with how good they are.

The second theory, called the model of limited resources, is relevant to the jealousy and rivalry between friends and siblings.

We know through history that people lived close to starvation. They viewed every member of the family and their friends as competitors. Since the resources were limited, jealousy was a common sight and thus, evolved in us humans and persists to this day.

Of course, many other reasons make one jealous. For example, there is abandonment, betrayal, or loss. When a partner finds out that they have been cheated on, they expect to be betrayed again. The fear of abandonment, hurt, and betrayal prevents them from establishing deep and meaningful relationships. They fear that the same would happen again and to somehow prevent it, they become overly possessive. They want to keep tabs on their partners at all times, want to know who they are spending their free time with and doing what. This inquisitiveness can drive the other partner away as they constantly feel judged.

Then, there is your attachment style. How you connect with others tells a lot about you too. People who avoid commitment or closeness don't get jealous as often as their partners because they value their autonomy more. They aren't there to form close relationships and this makes their partner feel unvalued and unimportant, leading to jealousy about how carefree their partner is.

Many partners are less jealous at the beginning of the relationship because they haven't invested themselves fully into it. However, as the relationship grows and becomes dearer, they become more jealous because, now, their investment in it has increased. They have more to lose now than they had before.

Next, is uncertainty which makes partners act out of jealousy. Partners that are in a long-distance relationship (LDR) often feel jealous. So do those that live in different time zones or have recently started something new and challenging in their lives. The uncertainty that comes with LDR, time zone differences, and new career pursuits, often results in couples spending less time with one another, thus failing to stay in touch. The constant fear that they are enjoying their lives without you while you stay miserable and alone breeds feelings of insecurity and jealousy. Any picture with friends on social media when they tell you they are too tired to talk can cause the other partner to feel betrayed and jealous. Then, partners, who are on different levels of commitment, i.e. one being super invested and the other just casually dating, can also become prone to jealousy from the partner that puts in too much in the relationship.

If you think that this relationship is essential to your happiness whereas the other partner doesn't feel so, it can also lead to some jealousy on your part. If one partner feels like they have no better alternatives, they will feel jealous if treated like they are replaceable. Also, if this relationship is the only support system you have, then fear of losing it can also make you extra cautious and jealous.

Jealousy also stems from low self-esteem. There is countless research that proposes that when one partner feels they aren't good enough for their partner, they tend to experience symptoms of jealousy. They feel replaceable and their inner critic keeps telling them that their partner can do so much better. Jealousy signals an imbalance in the relationship. It happens when one or both partners feels like they aren't good enough for the other.

Some people that are quick to jump to conclusions also become jealous easily. Let's call it the jealousy hijack. Ask yourself this: when you were jealous of your partner over something, what followed next? Was it not more negative feelings and threats that they might be out cheating behind your back? Were you not afraid that they would leave you? Did you not end up discounting the positives in the relationship? Our unrealistic assumptions that we deserve a fairytale can cloud our thinking. We dream of perfect romance and when our partner doesn't live up to it, we feel an aversion towards them.

Signs Your Partner Is Jealous

Moving forward, how can you spot some important signs that hint at jealousy in your partner and not the healthy kind? Below are some symptoms that are common in all jealous partners. You will notice that many are similar to that of a controlling partner but their expression and reasoning are different. Take a look!

They Want You All For Themselves

It's one thing to make sweeping statements to charm your partner and another to use them to trap your partner. If you are with someone that reminds you that no one can love you the way they do, or how others are unappreciative of your efforts, or how they would hate to share you with someone else, know that these are statements thinly veiled with jealousy. These may sound grand when you are dating them, even flattering, but they suggest underlying jealousy and insecurity. It is an attempt to control the relationship.

Know the difference between missing you and wanting to spend all the time with you. Unhealthy jealousy doesn't promise a healthy or lasting relationship.

They Check-In On You

Calling you when you aren't home, texting you all day, inquiring about your whereabouts and who you have been with, is another sign of unhealthy jealousy. If they get paranoid every time you are out of sight or busy with something other than them, what they have is unhealthy jealousy. This will leave you, as their partner, always anxious and worried every time you have to go somewhere important. They may even ask what you are doing, who else is with you, and at what time will you get free. If for some reason, you are late, they blame and accuse you of cheating.

They Have All Your Passwords

They monitor all your social media activities, demand that you share your passwords with them, posing it as transparency. They have an issue with who you follow and who follows you back, make a fuss every time someone likes your photo or sends a DM, even strangers. They make you put your profile private, and check your phone secretly whenever you aren't around. They go past your recent search history and demand an explanation when they find something suspicious. This is a complete breach of privacy. This shouldn't be allowed. If they keep tabs on you like this and present it as wanting to protect you or keep you safe, let them know how it makes you feel.

They Stalk People You Are In Touch With

If a distant cousin, a friend from school, teacher, or colleague likes a photo of you or leaves a comment, they go stalking who they are and what business they have from you. They want to know everything about everyone that reacts or comments on your posts. They do this because they assume you are cheating on them, which suggests a lack of trust. They become inquisitive about your friends, colleagues, and even cousins you only meet over holidays.

They Make You Download Tracking Apps On Your Phone

They keep tracking where you are at through apps they made you install on your phone. They don't trust you when you tell them that you are stuck in traffic and would check for themselves. They expect you to deliver immediate responses when out somewhere without them. Once you are home, they want a detailed explanation of your itinerary, minute-by-minute.

They Make Rules About Who You Can Talk To

If you steer clear of certain people because you know your partner will have an issue with it, it sounds like you are with someone that is both insecure and jealous. Remember in the example, how Adam had an issue when Julianne had a brief chat with her boss? Notice how jealous and insecure he became and made a fuss about it? If the same happens with you and you are made to explain yourself, it is time you accept that this is an unhealthy obsession. They shouldn't have a right to who you can talk to, especially when they have the right to do so. Of course, the list excludes exes, flirty co-workers, and people you had a crush on. When you ask them if they don't trust you, they tell you that it is them that they don't trust. They tell you that they have observed how a cousin, boss, or friend looks at you and how it upsets them.

They Don't Allow You To Have Fun Without Them

Every fun and exciting plan has to include them. Otherwise, they don't permit you. They make up excuses like, "But what will I do all alone at home, take me with you." This hints at their jealousy and lack of trust in you. They are afraid that you will be so happy that you won't come back to them. They fear that you will find someone better than them and therefore, want to be with you all the time.

They Pick A Fight When You Get Dressed

When you are about to go out, dressed for an event or business party, they pick up a petty fight with you over how you are dressed, why you have so much makeup on, what's with the dark shade of the lipstick, and the hair, etc. They want that you either don't go or feel like you are overdressed and tone down. The action is aimed at limiting or preventing any chance to meet anyone. They make you conscious of how you look so that you won't feel comfortable approaching anyone. Again, the goal is to isolate you from others and keep you all for yourself.

Jealousy adds tension to the relationship. When one partner remains constantly suspicious of the actions of others, even though they are harmless, it has little to do with you and more with the issues they are dealing with. They don't do it purposely, they have been through some events that clouded their judgment and caused hurt. Therefore, they don't want the same to happen again, and therefore, act jealous.

But their jealousy might take a toll on you too. It can take away the freedom you have or had before you met them. You can feel policed and like a criminal all the time when you have to answer their probing questions. You can feel like in a cage when your social life is being stalked and paraded into. This tension will affect how you see them. It will affect your mental and emotional peace. It will give rise to conflicts and disagreements. It will take away all the fun from the relationship and you will feel stuck.

What Can You Do About It

Remember, when jealousy gets the best of the relationship, it can never thrive. So what can you do to help your partner treat you like an equal, trust you, and not take over your life and personal space? Here are some ideas you can work with.

Effective communication with your partner about their insecurities and fears can be a good start. You want to be in their shoes and see the world from their eyes. What breeds this insecurity? Why can't they control their obsessive nature? What can you say or do that will make them trust you more? These are all great questions to talk about. The idea is to get to the root of the issue and know how you can help them recover. However, don't try to fix, negate, or minimize their reasons. That would be bullying them into submission. Talk; simply talk without any humiliating, shameful, or threatening remarks. Let them confide in you. Show empathy and let them know that they have your undivided attention.

Transparency is a must. All relationships require honest partners. When there is jealousy from one of the partners, you both can sit down and make rules about how you want to proceed with the relationship, what activities you have to be transparent about, what is allowed and what isn't, who can you talk to, and under what circumstances does one have to tell the other about their whereabouts. For example, if one of you decides to make plans with a friend or co-worker, you must let your partner know beforehand. Such clear rules will minimize the instances of jealousy and help your partner trust you. Similarly, you can also decide to share or not share passwords to social media accounts. If you think this will help your partner alleviate the anxiety they experience when they are in the unknown, do it.

If your partner feels like you are the only friend and companion in their lives, they are going to demand more attention and love. They will want to do fun things with you and fight when you don't feel the same. Stress on the importance of having a life outside of the relationship. If their world keeps revolving around you, they are going to come back to you for everything. Therefore, encourage them to stay in touch with their friends too. Motivate them to make plans for the weekend with their family and friends. The less time they spend with you, the less worried they will be. This will give them something to focus on and not depend on you for your time and attention.

He Wants To Stay In Contact 24/7

"I SAW THE WAY you looked at them and laughed. You never seem this happy with me."

This comment bugged Sarah the most. Richard always had this issue. He always felt insecure. He felt like he wasn't good enough or didn't love Sarah enough. He always thought that she was unhappy with him. Despite her telling him a hundred times that this wasn't the case, she had realized that there was no pleasing Richard. She could never assure him that his love was enough. She could never assure him that she had never been this happy in her life. Her words, promises, and guarantees, always fell short because there was no convincing Richard.

He had picked up the same charade today after they returned from a wedding. It was Sarah's cousin's wedding and she was meeting her extended family after a year or so. Of course, her happiness was evident. But this didn't please Richard at all. He kept noticing how radiant her smile was, how genuine she seemed, how carefree her actions were. She seemed to be having the best time of her life. He recalled the dinner the other night where she *had kept quiet and reserved throughout the night. Was he not able to make her happy? Did she feel no spark in their relationship anymore?*

Was she going to leave me?

Is your partner the same? Does he always keep fishing for compliments? Does he often ask you where you are headed, even though they know the answer? Do they still badger you for extra attention when they have spent the entire day with you? Do they frequently question your love towards them? Are they worried that you will leave them for someone better? Do they create a fuss when you talk to someone else, even at a public gathering? Are they always worried that people are gossiping about them?

Many partners feel insecure when it comes to relationships. Although their partner loves them unconditionally, they still worry that they don't.

Insecurity in relationships is a lot like jealousy. However, jealousy is only an aspect of it. Insecurity is an inner feeling that has more to do with the person experiencing it rather than the partner. Insecure partners feel threatened all the time. They experience feelings of self-doubt and assume that their partner isn't loyal towards them or will leave them. This constant fear sabotages the beautiful relationship they have. It prevents partners from connecting emotionally on the same level as one of them always craves surety. Chronic anxiety can rob couples of peace and minimizes the chances of establishing a promising relationship. The actions and behaviors often associated with insecurity make it impossible for the other partner to continue. Insecure partners need reassurance, can act jealous, accuse, and snoop around, eroding trust. The other partner feels like they are always judged, under scrutiny, and not untrustworthy.

Most insecurity comes from within us. Insecure partners feel unloved and unsure of their partners. They can't control themselves from judging their every move and spying on them. They constantly check on them, demand reassurance of loyalty, and suffer from poor self-esteem. The majority of this insecurity is based on irrational thoughts and fears. There are many causes or reasons behind the depiction of such behavior.

The first most common reason for relationship insecurity is a negative past. We have all walked away from relationships that looked promising. The partner ended up breaking our trust, lying, or cheating. This scared us. We become fearful that something similar would happen to us again. Partners who think the same are unable to establish deep connections even when the current partner is all giving and deserving of love. They view them with the same suspicion and can't believe that they will remain faithful. Thus, the constant questioning and inspection.

Then some partners haven't gotten over their past and are still carrying the emotional baggage with them. They bring it into their current relationship. Those unresolved issues from the past keep coming back to bite in the tush and create insecurity. Those partners end up projecting the same hate and jealousy they felt for their previous partner, onto their current ones. They subconsciously keep holding onto the remorse they feel and let it be inflicted on their current partner.

Some insecure partners also suffer from poor self-esteem and lack of confidence. This can be traced back to their childhood where they were either bullied or constantly reminded that they aren't good enough. Those negative experiences had a long-term effect on their personality. When such feelings remain unresolved, they can continue into adulthood as well. The resulting outcome remains unchanged. They still feel insecure because of the type of conditioning they received.

Next, your attachment style also determines the kind of partner you become (secure or insecure). According to the theory of attachment, children who don't receive love and attention from their partners grow up to be insecure. Coming from a neglected childhood, their emotional needs remain unmet. Therefore, when they meet someone ready to fulfill those needs, they don't know what to make of it and how to act accordingly, as they have been deprived of it all their life.

Finally, we also see some partners lose their identities after they meet someone and start a new relationship with them. They lose their sense of personal life fulfillment and rely on their partners for it. They take up hobbies and interests of their partners, hoping that this would help them get closer to them. However, the minute they put their happiness in their partner's lap and rely on them to provide fulfillment, the same minute they become insecure. Relying on someone else to add meaning to life is unhealthy as we all are unique. We must never forget that what got our partner interested in us was our uniqueness. They felt attracted to the qualities you had. They felt attracted because they didn't possess the same attributes. Losing them is a big mistake.

Signs Your Partner Is Insecure

It is often difficult to distinguish between jealous, controlling, and insecure partners. Their symptoms seem to coincide. They all want to control your life, manipulate you into doing things; check in with you all the time, keep tabs on your whereabouts and demand your attention. However, some traits are unique to insecure partners. For instance, they don't trust you easily. They doubt all your actions, stalk your social media accounts to see what you are up to, check your phone behind your back, snoop on you and when you ask them why they do it, they feel threatened. They become defensive and put the blame on you for not being transparent enough.

They Don't Have A Social Life
Insecure partners are also insecure about who they are. Therefore, they avoid big gatherings and have small social circles. They rarely hang out with their friends or make plans to see them. They don't have any passionate hobbies either. They avoid places where they can pursue new friendships like gyms, bars, or social events. Since they have nowhere to go and no one to talk to, they want to spend all of their time with you and expect you to feel the same. When you fail to show interest or reciprocate their feelings, they fear abandonment and act more insecure.

They Need Constant Validation
They are never happy about how they look. They crave validation and attention all the time. They fish for compliments. They want to be praised as it boosts their self-esteem. However, no amount of compliments and praises are enough. No matter how many times you reassure them of how they look or how much you love them, they still want more.

This never-ending hunger for compliments and praises can make you feel helpless. You feel like you have a job to do.

They Feel Attacked Easily

Since they believe everything is about them, they get offended easily. You can't tell them to do something they don't want to do because to them, that's crossing a line. However, they can do the same to you because it is their right. They know very well how to emotionally shut down when you expect something from them in return. If you demand answers, they view it as criticism. If you raise your voice or are slightly sarcastic, suddenly the whole conversation changes to how you could use that tone with me. If you remind them that they haven't done something you expected them to do, instead of taking the blame and accepting their fault, they become hurt and act defensively.

They Create Issues Out Of Everything

Talk about creating mountains out of molehills! They have many issues with the way you say something, how you dress, where you are going, why are you hanging out with your friends and family, why you don't want to stay at home watching Netflix together, etc. They use accusations and definitive words to remind you that you are in the wrong for wanting something just for yourself. They find things to fight about when you are in a good mood, only to spoil it. They create a fuss over small issues like why the laundry isn't folded right, why you were talking to the delivery man, why you called your mother, etc.

They Represent Themselves As Victims

Whenever they talk about their past relationship, they represent themselves as the victims. They talk badly about their ex. They have not one positive thing to say about them. This is a trick to make you feel like you owe yourself to them. They act like victims to get more love, compliments, and praises from you. They do it so that you will feel sympathy for them and remain faithful.

They Don't Take Criticism Well

You can't guilt-trip them because they just can't tolerate criticism. Whenever you have something negative to point out about their behavior, they feel disappointed and ensure that you know it. They act all disheartened, tell you that they probably deserve the hate and that they aren't good enough for you so that you can console them and take back your remarks.

They Don't Like Being Talked About

Whenever you are in a public place or social event with them, they try to make everything about themselves. They think that everyone there is talking about them. They feel eyed upon. They think others are gossiping about them and it bothers them. They don't let you enjoy and stick by your side all night and then complain about how awful they felt about going there.

They Don't Like Themselves

They aren't confident about their looks and physique. They think they aren't handsome or smart enough. Even when they are dressed their best, they feel like something is missing. Your compliments don't make them feel better either. There is just assuring them. As they have poor self-esteem, they judge themselves too harshly. They hold themselves to high standards and whenever they fail to live up to them, they feel disheartened.

What Can You Do About It

Having studied their unique behavior and how they use their insecurity to guilt you into proving your love over and over again, here's what you can do to help them recover from those feelings of insecurity and learn to trust you and your actions over time.

Make an effort to keep the spark of love alive. Just because the relationship is a year or two old doesn't mean you stop making efforts to sustain it. Insecurity stems when a partner feels like the love is fading. They feel like the magic is gone. Be creative. Plan surprises. Appreciate their smallest gestures so that they know that you still feel blessed to have them in your life. Bring back that same passion you two shared between yourselves when you started dating. Act like you are newbies in love again. Revisit the places that mean something to you. Compliment them frequently. Leave them love notes to wake up to. You won't believe the power such small gestures hold.

Secondly, talk about the unmet needs that cause them to react a certain way. As humans, we all have six basic needs. We all feel a certain way to gain pleasure and avoid pain. We all crave variety in life. We want a connection with others. We want to feel significant. We want to grow and contribute to seeking fulfillment in life. Ask your partner which of these needs he thinks he lacks and work on it. If they say they feel there is no connection between you two, build one. If they feel insignificant in the relationship, start to appreciate and compliment them more. If they say they crave variety in love, opt for creative and unique ways to spend your time together.

For example, pick up a new hobby, enroll in a weekend class, go on an unplanned trip, try a new cuisine, etc.

Finally, the third thing that you can do is ask your partner to create a list of all the things they are fearful of about the relationship. These can include, lack of trust, dishonesty, lack of transparency and attention, etc. Once a list of reasons has been jotted down, go through each of them separately and come up with solutions together. For instance, if they are insecure about the way you talk to other guys, make an effort to minimize your interactions with guys when they are with you. If you are all going out together, give your partner more attention so that they don't feel left out. Similarly, to combat a lack of trust, promise to call/text them when there is a change of plan and keep them posted about where you are and what you are doing. That way, they will remain relieved and not make a fuss.

HE KEEPS CHECKING MY PHONE AND ASKING WHERE I AM

Robert: I just saw you do it again!

Robert: There is a miscall at 15:20 from an unknown number. Who called you?

Jen: I don't know, let me see...

Jen: Oh, that was someone from an insurance company wanting me to buy some package.

Robert: Are you sure?

Jen: Who else would it be?

Robert: I don't know. You tell me.

Jen: I just told you.

Jen: Wait...what are you doing?

Robert: I am just calling the number to make sure you are telling the truth.

Jen: Are you insane, it's past midnight!

Robert: Then tell me the truth, who called you?

Jen: Why would I lie about it? You can call them tomorrow to check for yourself. Just cut the call for now.

Robert: Jen, tell me who called you? Was it Andrew?

Jen: Andrew, my ex, Andrew? Why would he call me?

Robert: I don't know, you tell me!

Jen: Oh my god, I am not doing this again. Not tonight. I have to reach the office early tomorrow.

Robert: Oh, so are you going on a date now?

Jen: Please stop, just stop!

Jen was exhausted and angry. There was no pleasing Robert. He had trust issues that run so deep that nothing she said was going to reassure him that it was just a call from the insurance company and not from an ex-boyfriend she dumped. Robert was becoming obsessive and controlling day by day. He demanded explanations from her but never believed them. He was sure that she was lying to him and going behind his back to meet and flirt with someone else.

What could she do to make him believe that he was the only one in her life? Was there any way to put an end to this misery and interrogation that made Jen feel humiliated?

Emotional intimacy is the hallmark of a loving and close relationship. It can involve sharing personal information as well as vulnerable secrets. However, there is a limit to what can be shared and must be shared and this classification is different for every couple. It should be up to you two to decide what boundaries you want to set in the relationship and what to do when one tries to invade them.

Some partners don't understand the difference between privacy and secrecy. They think that if the partner isn't telling them everything, they are hiding it. However, the other partner might not feel so. They might simply think that it isn't significant enough to talk about.

This misinterpretation can blur the line between privacy and secrecy.

Spying on your partner, snooping in their phone, or requiring constant disclosure shouldn't be allowed. It breaks the rules of personal space that one is entitled to, even when they are in a committed relationship. They should have the right to keep some things private. When partners openly demand that everything must be told to them and snoop around secretly, it suggests that they are suspicious.

They don't trust your word or actions and violate your privacy because they think you are keeping secrets from them. They do petty things like checking your messages and call logs when you are out of the room, reading through your conversations on WhatsApp, stalking all those that comment or react to your posts and pictures on social media, etc. Some go as far as checking their partner's internet history to ensure they haven't been engaging with other people on different websites without them knowing. This lack of trust in the partner can leave the partner feeling judged and scrutinized.

Such behavior tells you one of the following things.

- They have unresolved trust issues. They were probably cheated on and therefore, think that it will happen to them again. Research shows that partners who were cheated on are more suspicious of their current partner. It makes sense. If you had been cheated on before and didn't see the signs, your common sense tells you to be vigilant the next time. You have been through the hurt and know how much time it takes to get over someone and you don't want to experience anything remotely as close as that. So you become extra cautious and want to be closer to your current partner. You want to know what they have been doing all day, who they've been engaging with, and why they take so much time to respond when they are online and available to chat on their Facebook account. Therefore, they need reassurance from time to time that they won't be cheated upon again. They need reassurance that they won't have to endure the same pain again. They want to be reassured that they will get their happy ending.

- Secondly, they act suspicious because the communication between you two is poor. For any relationship to remain healthy, both parties must practice honesty and openness with one another. If your partner feels like you are hiding something from them, they are bound to feel isolated and suspicious. If they don't get a proper reply from you, they are going to go looking for it themselves. When they believe that you are deliberately not responding to their inquiries and avoiding answering, it encourages snooping. Therefore, poor communication between partners can make matters worse and give rise to suspicion and snooping. Conversely, if you and your partner communicate actively and love to share your day's events, there is no need for snooping around. This can improve trust in one another and diminish the instances of suspicion from their end.

- Finally, they might snoop around when they suspect that you are cheating on them or are no longer committed to the relationship. This fear usually arises when they notice that you are no longer the same person you were at the start of the relationship. You seem distant and unappreciative. You avoid spending time with them and prefer to enjoy your weekends with your friends. You make up excuses for not returning home on time or forget important events. Of course, you might not be doing it on purpose and be stressed due to work or any other commitment, but to them, it feels like you are cheating on them. So they snoop around to make sure that their fears aren't true and the relationship is as it was before.

Signs Your Partner Is Suspicious

Suspicion and lack of trust can destroy even the most perfect of relationships. When one partner starts to believe that the other is hiding something, lying to them, or worse, cheating on them, it can take away one's mental and emotional peace. It can even end with the partners separating because both of them are tired of explaining to one another how they feel about each other's actions. Holding onto suspicious feelings and not expressing them with your partner can build up and lead to frustration. This buildup of suppressed feelings eventually pours out in the worst of ways, leaving the other partner startled and feelings accused.

Speaking about the signs of suspicious jealousy, they are no different than the ones we have already talked about. There is checking of the phone, snooping around, stalking, wanting to know all the deets, and looking through personal belongings like smelling the perfume on the shirt, trying to find a lipstick mark or hair strand on your partner's clothes, etc. However, some are unique to an insecure and suspicious partner. An active imagination, for starters, is unique. Most suspicious partners have an active imagination where they think the worst of their partners. For example, if they are a tad bit late in arriving home, they assume they are banging someone in a cheap motel. If they are taking their phone to the loo with them, they suspect that they are sending dirty texts to their mistress and can't wait to get hold of their phone. If they don't find any suspicious messages, they assume that their partner has deleted them.

They Accuse You Of Lying

Other than that, suspicious partners also accuse their partners of lying. The lack of trust is evident in their words and behaviors. They tell you that they don't trust you or that you are lying, straight in your face. Even when you answer all their questions, they doubt your answers, because, in their mind, they have already established you as a liar.

They Ask You The Same Questions Repeatedly

It is one thing to know where you were at a certain time of the day and another to ask the same question at different intervals throughout the day. There is no convincing a suspicious partner. No matter how hard you try to reassure them that you aren't lying or making up stuff, they are going to think that you are. Asking the same questions, again and again, is their way of testing them to see if you would switch up your responses and they will have the chance to prove that you are a liar.

They Keep Checking For Receipts

Telling them where you spent your money today doesn't sit fine with them. They have to check it for themselves. So they would dig into your wallet and look at the receipts of what you bought, ate, or paid. This also indicates a lack of trust in you because they don't take your word for it. They will look at your credit card statements and match debited and credited amounts to the dates they were deposited or credited. If you have been out of town, they confirm your bookings before your visit and check in with you while you are there to ensure you are not anywhere else.

They Can Be Accusatory

They can begin to accuse you of simple things that you haven't even done, like leaving them for another man without any evidence to back their words. They notice your behaviors and use that knowledge against you. For example, if they noticed you talking to someone at a party, even if just casually, they would create a fuss about it once you are home. They will say things like you were probably asking for his number or wishing that you could go up to his place for the night. This is their way of demanding more attention and wanting to protect themselves by preempting any chance of betrayal by raising suspicions at you.

They Don't Let You Around Attractive People

Lack of trust is also evident from the fact that they try to push you away from people they think are attractive. They think you will try to flirt with them and get frisky. So they make every attempt to be by your side when you are out and demand that you hold their hand, and remain glued. They glance at anyone angrily looking your way, even when you don't notice.

They Seek Confirmations

If you say you are with your friends, they demand to speak to one of them just to confirm your story. If you say you are at a party with co-workers, they request you to send pictures and name everyone in the picture. If you say you were out with a family member, they will call that family member just to confirm that they were with you and ask trick questions as to what you two did, where you ate, when did you leave, etc. to make sure that your story checks out.

They Are Inquisitive About Your Ex

They keep bringing up your ex in different everyday conversations. It isn't to hurt you specifically but to know how you still feel about them. If they sense that your heart has softened towards them, they accuse you of staying in touch with your ex or still having feelings for him.

What Can You Do About It

So how can this be prevented and remedied? Although effective communication and showing love and affection seem to work well, there are some other ideas to prevent suspicion from your partner and reassure them of your love and devotion to them.

First up, be as detailed as possible when discussing with them how your day went. Since you know they notice time gaps, make sure to include timestamps in your conversations. For example, you can tell them that you had lunch at two and then attended a meeting until four. Then you wrapped up your day's work, signed off at five, and were on your way back home at around fifteen past five. This will leave no room for suspicion. It's better if you can offer more information like what you had for lunch, what was discussed during the presentation, who else was with you in the elevator when you signed off from work, etc. Similarly, if there is a sudden change of plan, make sure that they are on board with it. If it involves family, ask them to come so that they don't feel excluded and later blame you for not thinking of calling you. The idea is to be as open as possible with them so that they don't become suspicious.

Secondly, avoid getting defensive all of a sudden. When you are dealing with an insecure, jealous, and suspicious partner, you have to deal with them with patience. You have to pass all rounds of interrogation with relaxation without getting offended. You also must listen calmly instead of getting defensive and irritated. Cutting them off prematurely or reacting with a careless and impatient gesture can blow up the situation. Moreover, it will give your partner a further reason to suspect your action. Another thing you must do is try not to dismiss or discount their feelings. Don't show exhaustion or reply with mean comments like, "Not again..." This will only make them feel more misunderstood. Listen to what they have to say and respond calmly. If they feel assured, they will stop questioning you.

Finally, have mutual friends. Become friends with their friends and encourage them to do the same with your friends. Mutual friends can serve as a great medium to reconcile your relationship. Your partner will feel more at ease when they know you are with someone they can trust completely. In case there is some misunderstanding, your friends can help clear it out and cover for you when needed.

HE THINKS I WILL LEAVE HIM FOR ANOTHER MAN

Caleb: I told you I didn't want to wear those shoes. One of my socks was torn at the toe. Everyone saw it at dinner.

Arianna: Relax, Caleb, the tear was on the back of the sock. I am sure no one saw it.

Caleb: Oh, I shouldn't have listened to you. If only you had allowed me to dress the way I wanted to.

Arianna: Had you dressed the way you wanted to, it would have looked like a formal tie event. It was a casual barbeque at my house, with my family.

Caleb: What must they be thinking about me! Look at Caleb; he doesn't even have decent socks.

Arianna: You are just overreacting. Everyone was wearing flip-flops. I told you to wear yours too. But no, it would have looked super casual according to you.

Caleb: I hope your mom didn't see it.

Arianna: I am sure she didn't. Besides, she adores you. Even if she saw, it wouldn't have changed her views about you. They all love you for who you are, not how you dress or act. They consider you family, so just chill!

Arianna had a difficult time convincing Caleb that his sock tear was just something that happened. It could have happened to anyone. Not a big deal! But to him, everything was a big deal. Wanting to take him somewhere was a disaster. He always felt like people were gossiping about him, talking about his creased shirt, poor choice of color for the suit, sneakers, and hairstyle. He was sure that Arianna would leave him for another much smarter, handsome, and richer partner. He often says the same to her and spends the whole day with a frown on his face.

He was indecisive and needed everyone's opinion before buying something as simple as a tie. He didn't think of himself as presentable, deserving of Arianna, or even be loved.

Was there any way Arianna could convince Caleb that he was perfect just as he was and that he didn't have to work extra hard to impress her and her family and friends?

Lack of confidence and poor self-esteem can result in relationship anxiety. Relationship anxiety can be defined as having feelings of insecurity and doubt about your partner even when the relationship is progressing smoothly. Worrying that your partner will leave you for someone better, thinking that you aren't good enough, reading too much into your partner's actions and words, questioning yourself if your presence makes them happy or not, doubting their feelings for you, and wondering if you matter to them at all, are all signs of relationships anxiety.

When you imagine someone with low self-esteem, you imagine them as shy, an introvert, or someone that can't hold conversations like others. It can be someone who is always worried about their looks, wondering what others are thinking about them, or always saying negative things about themselves. When it comes to romantic relationships, this can affect them destructively and cause arguments and imbalance.

Signs Your Partner Has Low Self-Esteem

Partners who are unable to put their needs forth in front of their partners and suffer silently have low self-esteem. They have a tough time asking their partner for something because to them, it seems too inconveniencing or burdening. For instance, if they have to move stuff, they would rather call a removalist firm than their friends because they feel shy. In romantic relationships, they also put their partner's needs first and therefore, never feel fully content because their needs remain unattended.

They Are Jealous And Insecure

Partners who suffer from poor self-esteem also tend to act insecure and jealous about their significant other. They have this never-ending fear that their partner will be attracted to someone else and leave. As a response, they act clingy and crave attention all the time. When the partner fails to fulfill their request to be on their call 24/7, they assume terrible conclusions that further put their partner off.

They Seek Approval Constantly

They can never be themselves because they always strive to be someone better than themselves. They want to be praised and appreciated. They seek validation and approval from everyone they meet. They have this unending urge to please everyone which prevents them from being who they really are.

This can also not sit right with you because you want them to be completely honest and pure when with you. You don't want an upgraded, always charming, or having high standards for themselves.

They Allow Others To Walk Over Them

They rarely have any opinions of their own because they want to please others and go with what they are saying or doing. This can lead to boredom for you as their partner as you would want them to open up and contribute in conversations. Since they have a hard time expressing themselves, they let others walk all over them. When they are betrayed or taken advantage of by others, they become extremely emotional and hard to comfort. Their reliance and dependency on you also become permanent.

They Go Beyond To Fulfill The Needs Of Their Partner

Expect them to shower you with gifts, compliments, and surprises because they think that is how they can keep you engaged and interested in them. They will go to any lengths to please you. They go extravagant just so that you can stay in love with them. Even when they know that the relationship isn't going anywhere, they don't have the guts to call it off and will continue to be in it despite it draining their energy.

They Need Reassurance

They request your approval for everything whether it is ordering food or planning a trip to your family over the weekend. It may seem loving at first that they value your opinion, however, as time passes by, you start to wish that they would decide something for once themselves. Their continuous need for reassurance can make you feel like you have to prove your love to them all the time. They also keep asking you about your feelings for them but don't seem reassured when you tell them. It's a never-ending conversation where neither party leaves happy.

Since these signs indicate a lack of self-worth, what they need is a partner that can reassure them of their love. They want someone that acts and feels confident in establishing a long-term relationship with them. What they need is someone that would help work on them and support them in gaining that confidence they lack. If you are with someone that seems unsure of who they are, it can be a bit challenging to prove your love over and over again. It can feel like you are on a pedestal every other day, proclaiming your love for them. It might feel easy and natural at the start of the relationship but as you gradually progress towards something more solid, it can feel like a chore. It can also be disheartening to see when they don't think of themselves as deserving of all the good things and are always focused and worried about getting better.

What Can You Do About It

What you can do is help them address their needs for starters. What is it that they truly want out of the relationship? How can you as a partner improve? Do they need more attention, love, or closeness? Do they wish you could be intimate with their family? Once they can communicate their needs and exhibit what according to them, is a promising relationship, you both can work together to address those needs. Make an effort to show that you care about them too. You can always start small. For instance, if they wish there was more physical closeness in the relationship, you can start with random hugs and kisses throughout the day. You can plan date nights or movie nights if they want to spend more time with you doing fun stuff. You can show an interest in their work if they wish you would care about what they do, etc. If they wish you stay in touch more with their family, schedule meet-ups, and phone calls with them.

Next, notice and appreciate the little things that he does for you to boost his morale. Even if it is as simple as helping you around the kitchen while you cook, getting the groceries from the car, opening the door for you when you leave for work, or saving you snacks while watching TV. Start noticing and appreciating these little efforts that he puts in to ensure that your needs are taken care of. Say things like how happy and blessed you are to have them as your partner, or how caring and devoted they are. These may not matter to you but they will matter to them and help them gain self-confidence. Your words will make them feel worthy of what they have and value themselves as they should. It will improve their self-worth and how they feel about themselves.

Show consistent support in what they do. This is taking another step from complimenting to reciprocating their behaviors and gestures. If you find them struggling with something, buzz in to offer moral support. Let them know that you trust them to figure it out since they are so smart and creative. If they are having trouble with a chore, offer to help out. If you can't help them mentally or physically, show your support emotionally. For instance, if they want to lose weight and haven't been able to, praise their efforts for trying so hard instead of telling them that they need to try extra hard. Offer recommendations like taking a walk together after dinner or do yoga early in the morning together to get them started. Your support and appreciation will help them overcome the negativity they have inside. They will start to view themselves in a positive light and feel capable of doing anything they set their mind to.

HE KEEPS LYING TO ME

JACK WAS THE ONE responsible for mailing the bills. He always needs some extra pushing from Nancy to ensure that he did it. However, recently, with the baby and new motherhood, Nancy had other things to focus on. She did recall telling him about the bills arriving two weeks ago and he had put them in the car, promising to mail them before going to work. She thought he had. However, today, she had received a call from the bank stating that they were behind and would be charged an extra $200 as a late fee. But Jack had said that he had mailed them already?

Why did he lie? As frustrated as Nancy was with Jack and his never-ending lies, it got her thinking if there were other things that he had lied about recently? He had been coming back from work late every night and anxiety started to seep inside her head. Why did he have to make things this difficult? Why could he not be honest about things with her?

Lying comes naturally. We all can attest to telling lies every other day. For example, telling someone that their tie looks good when it looks hideous and doesn't go with the outfit, pretending to have the flu to skip work, staying until late with our friends, and blaming it on the traffic when confronted, etc. Sometimes, lies seem so real that there is no way one would suspect them to be one.

But when we talk about intimate relationships, lying is something partners should avoid at all costs. Emotional honesty serves as the foundation for all relationships. It can be a deal-breaker when one partner is caught in a web of lies because it makes the other partner question every word they have ever said to them. Lying is often a deception that involves vague and ambiguous statements. It can also mean telling half-truths. It can mean exaggerating information or manipulating it to suit your needs. It can also include withholding valuable information that our partner has a right to know. For example, in our case above, had Jack told Nancy that he had forgotten about mailing the bills and they were still in his car, she wouldn't have begun to question all his motives. She would have reacted differently, perhaps, shown some anger but eventually would have understood and forgiven him. But now, the situation is different. Not only was she angry and frustrated, but she also felt unvalued. She felt taken advantage of. She felt betrayed by the one person she was supposed to trust the most.

Lies deprive the person of the freedom of choice and informed action. It is a clear violation of trust and a breach of one's kindness and devotion. Some lies are benign and well-intended like telling your partner that they don't look fat when they ask if they have gained some is a type of well-intended lie. The reasoning behind this is to boost your partner's morale and not hurt their feelings. However, some lies are a deliberate attempt to cause pain like covering up an alleged extramarital affair from your partner. You know from the minute you lie that if caught, it will hurt your partner. Yet, you go with it until caught. Most partners that lie do so for many reasons.

Partners lie because they want to protect their partner's feelings. Sometimes, they know that telling the truth will hurt your feelings, and therefore, they don't disclose the real reason behind an action. For example, if they know that your family is mean to you and doesn't deserve the love and attention you give them, they might come up with excuses that will prevent you from going. They may do so because they have seen you coming back feeling low and sad and don't want you to feel the same again.

Another reason partners lie is because they want to avoid conflicts and arguments, especially when they have done something that would start one. They don't want to face the consequences and therefore make up lies to cover up the truth. We saw a similar case with Jack who had lied to Nancy about mailing the bills. He knew that if he told her that he hadn't mailed them, she would have gotten angry and started a fight. He didn't want that and therefore lied.

Thirdly, partners lie because they fear that if they tell the truth, there is a chance that their partner or spouse would leave them. Hiding an affair, lying about a past relationship, or about staying in touch with their ex is a kind of lie that can land partners in hot waters. They know that if they are caught, their partners will leave them. So they tell lies after lies to keep repeating the same behavior and not getting caught.

Then, partners also lie because they don't want you to find out their flaws. This is most common when couples start dating. They would lie about liking the same sports, loving the same genre of music and shows, just because they want to connect with their partners better. They also lie about their personality, interests, and hobbies because they don't want to come off as boring and lose a potential partner because of it. They may also hide things or not be transparent about things relating to them like past relationships, childhood, job, and family, etc. so that their partner isn't freaked out or put off.

Next, partners lie because they want to maintain control of a situation. In our case study of Jack and Nancy, Jack thought that he would mail the bills when he had the time. He could have asked Nancy to mail them as it was near their place but he wanted to be the one to mail them. He wanted to maintain control but he messed up.

Partners can also lie to one another when they want to show off how talented, special, and successful they are. They may lie about their job, salary, relationship with their family, and their interests to keep their partner intrigued. They lie because they want to make themselves appear good and desirable. They exaggerate facts so that their partner thinks that they are a worthy catch and they maintain their control over the relationship.

Finally, partners lie because they want to postpone making a lifestyle change. For example, your partner may have lied about giving up smoking because you didn't like it. However, they continue to smoke when they are at the office or with their friends without your knowledge. Similarly, they can lie about controlling their diet or eating healthy when they are trying to lose weight but still enjoy steaks and burgers when ordering lunch at the office.

The most obvious impact lying can have on a relationship is the erosion of trust. In this date and time, it is so hard to find someone you can rely on, trust, and share your secrets with. Having trust go out of the window, there isn't much left to hold on to. When one partner feels like they can no longer trust the other, they can't remain sincere. Things can't proceed if one keeps thinking they are being lied to about everything. Therefore, it is important to read between the lines and discover when you are being lied to. Then, you can confront your partner and demand an explanation. It can also help you understand why they lie and what they get out of it.

Signs Your Partner Is Being Dishonest

According to several relationship coaches and marriage mediators, many signs suggest when you are being lied to. These signs are scientifically proven and easy to spot if one knows where to look.

Their Actions Don't Match Their Words

For starters, they don't end up living to the promises they made. There is an inconsistency between their words and actions. This can be a red flag. For example, they tell you that they will show more care or spend more time with you but their actions and behavior communicate the opposite entirely. They are still making plans with their friends and not helping out with the chores. There is no effort visible from their end to improve things.

They Take Long To Respond

When you speak your mind, you are usually quick and decisive. When you don't, you need more time expressing your thoughts because you are making them right there. Therefore, if you spot your partner always searching for the right words or editing their thoughts while speaking to you, know that they are lying.

Their Answers Are Exaggerated

Have you noticed that their explanations and stories always have these unnecessary elaborations? It's like they are trying hard to sell what they are saying so that there remain no loopholes. If you are in doubt, ask yourself this: how would you have responded to the same question? Would you have gone into the details of every second and not just briefly ended the story by highlighting the main ideas? Everyone would do that. However, when they go into exaggerated details, they are just making them as they go.

Their Body Language Gives It Away

When people lie, they have the habit of touching their face, scratching their nose, pointing fingers at the other person, or appearing fidgety. They don't look you in the eye and seem nervous or closed off. If you have been noticing these signs in your partner recently, know that they are lying about something. You don't have to be flagrant about it. You can simply point out that you don't think what they are saying makes any sense and begin to cross-question.

They Contradict Themselves

Their stories don't match. If they tell you something, it is different from what they tell someone else at another time. They get the dates or timing wrong and mess up the details. It makes you wonder if any of it makes sense because earlier, they had their facts all different. If you notice any inconsistencies in their stories like saying they were somewhere at a certain time and then when repeating the same story another day saying they were home by that time, you know something is fishy. They have made up a story to hide the truth from you and are having trouble remembering it. Good thing you don't have to remember the truth.

They Make Excuses

Have they been turning the tables on you recently whenever you question them about something? Suddenly, they put on the defensive mode and accuse you of not trusting them. They tell you how it hurts. Go back and re-examine the excuses they gave you when you asked them about something. Recall how they fabricated those excuses to cover up their tracks. For example, if they arrive late to a party, they blame it on the traffic, a tire blowout, lost keys, or last-minute changes to an important presentation that had to go out today. They simply avoid telling the truth and admit that they caused the delay because liars never accept their faults.

What Can You Do About It

Being the partner that is lied to frequently isn't the best place to be in. However, there are reasons why partners lie, men in particular. It's mostly because of the type of reaction they receive when they tell the truth. We all mess up. But we like to be forgiven. We don't want to be reminded of our faults in every conflict that happens. Women do that. They have the habit of bringing something up from the past when they sense they are losing the battle. I am not against this but if you are the man in the position, you wish you would have lied.

This, however, doesn't mean that partners can lie whenever they want to get out of something. It still violates trust and makes the partner being lied to, unvalued. It is both insensitive and humiliating to have found out that you have been lied to whereas the liar doesn't accept their mistake.

So what can you do? How can you make your partner honest with you about things that are both simple and complex? How can you make sure that you can trust their word and rely on them for being completely honest with you? Below are some great ideas to get started.

Review the many lies he has told in the past. What type are they? Does he lie because he wants to paint himself in a good light? Does he lie because he wants to avoid a subject? Does he lie because he is embarrassed or ashamed of where he comes from, a past relationship, or his career? Does he lie because he is afraid of your reaction and doesn't want to deal with it? Does he lie only under specific conditions or is he a compulsive liar?

Knowing what type of lies he makes up will help you understand where he is coming from and the reasons behind the lies. If it is out of habit, it might be a good start to talk to him about it. If he lies out of fear, you can reassure him that you will control your reactions and be patient while listening to him. Trying to understand his point of view will help you deal with the issue in a better light.

Next, reflect on your reactions. This is an important self-evaluation test. Contemplate your reactions when your partner speaks the truth after having lied to you first. If they come clean about something and your initial reaction involves arguments, name-calling, and abuse, then know that this is why he avoids telling the truth. What if he came up to you and asked you if he could go to his friend's house? What is your first reaction? Do you retaliate and argue about spending less time with you or do you happily allow him to go? Would you rather have him lie about an urgent chore like getting fuel for the car and then go to his friend's house behind your back?

Therefore, work on how you react when he tells you the truth. If he feels belittled, demeaned, and shamed every time he wants to do something for himself, he is going to start lying more and get away with it. In the end, it will be you getting hurt.

Lastly, ask him to repeat his story in reverse and see if he can. Asking direct questions as well as demanding him to tell his story in reverse will help you crack in the story. You see, lying takes effort. Retelling the story in the right chronological order but backward will lead to a fumble and assure you if they were lying about it. However, now that you have caught them red-handed, don't shame and blame them. Sit down and calmly inquire why they felt the need to lie and whether they have been doing it lately or not. If they genuinely care about you, they will share their reasons, and together, you can come up with a solution to avoid being lied to.

HE CHEATED...THIS IS THE END!

THERE SHE WAS, LYING on the bed, mourning her dead relationship. A friend had just sent her a picture of her spouse in a restaurant booth with another woman. Her name was Susan and she was his secretary. Lauren had met her when she once came to the house to drop off some important files Jordan had forgotten in the office. Lauren had instantly felt something odd about her. Her clothes were rather provocative for an office environment. She had full makeup on, gorgeous blonde hair, and heels that were at least 4-inch heels. But Jordon had barely looked at her once when receiving the files from her. She had watched because she felt intimidated by that woman's sexual aura.

Now, the reality was in front of her. No wonder Jordan had become so obsessed with his weight and appearance lately. He had been shaving quite often recently, even though Lauren loved the husky look on him. But he had been adamant about remaining clean-shaved because it looked more professional. The photo Lauren had received showed Jordan's hand caressing her hair and smiling at her in a way he hadn't smiled for months.

Suddenly, all of it was starting to make sense. Why he was always working late, why he was eating out more, why he was never at home even on weekends or had time for Lauren. She thought he was stressed about work and wanting to give her the best. She had shown her support throughout. They had also stopped having sex because he always complained about being tired.

What was she going to do now? Should she confront him? What was she going to say? Her body felt weak. Her head hurt. But most of all, it was her heart that ached as it had never before. This was the end. It has to be. Four years of togetherness, one beautiful daughter, and then this.

Discovering that you have been cheated on can be devastating. It can shatter your self-confidence. It can make you question all the things you ignored in the relationship because you were in love with your partner. It makes you question your self-worth and leaves you shocked. Feelings of anger, sadness, and hurt take over. You can't believe that you have been replaced so easily. You have invested so much in the relationship and this is what you have been rewarded for. It is cruel and unjust. You had heard about it happening to others but never thought you would be in the same boat one day.

Infidelity can be physically traumatic too. You feel like you have been punched in the gut and must now drown in your tears. You lose appetite or start binge-eating. You don't leave the house for days and stay isolated from the world. There is no comforting you. Despite being such a painful experience, you will be surprised to know that research suggests that more than 70% of people have thought about cheating on their partners whilst married. They have thought about casual sex with a stranger more often than you can imagine. They have created frisky scenarios in their heads about almost all men and women they meet, whom they find attractive. And this isn't just the men we are talking about. Women do it too. But several reasons trigger this urge. No one does it because they want to. There is always an unmet need that makes one want to wander around in search of it.

For instance, some partners run away from problems. They aren't the best communicators and can't deal with issues that arise. Therefore, instead of dealing with the issues at hand, they end up cheating on their spouses. The person they have an affair with is usually someone that understands them and is going through similar problems in their lives. Therefore, they connect on a mutual issue and become close.

Boredom can also cause some partners to cheat on their spouses. People have hectic routines, busy lives, and high expectations. This leaves little time for any form of excitement in their lives. This causes the relationship to suffer stagnancy and in hopes of finding some excitement and satisfaction in their lives, partners opt for something thrilling and new. A new intern at the office is exciting. A waiter that keeps bringing ketchup and napkins to your table is exciting. When partners want to break out of their busy lives and beat stagnancy, they seek new experiences that seem promising.

Then, some partners feel unwanted and unappreciated in the relationship. They feel that their partner doesn't give them enough time or is always complaining and nagging about the things they didn't do. Their opinions go unacknowledged, their words don't matter, and their feelings remain invalidated. This can make them feel unwanted and unvalued. They feel that their partner doesn't want them anymore and end up cheating on them. They cheat because they want that sense of control in their lives again. They want to be loved and taken care of. They want to know that someone thinks they are worthy. They cheat to boost their self-esteem and self-worth. Cheating makes them feel like they have still "got it."

Partners that are apart from one another for long durations also lack that connection that couples who live together have. Long-distance relationships often end because one or both partners got tired of being apart and ended up falling for someone else. This is one of the most common reasons for infidelity. Couples that are forced to live separately either due to the nature of their work or family commitments suffer from this. When one of them is missing for a long time, the other partner can feel lonely without anything keeping them busy. So they reach out to new people and activities, often stumbling upon like-minded people.

Some partners also complain of a lack of respect from their partners which urges them to seek it from elsewhere. Some partners feel disrespected when their words don't matter or their partner is too busy to notice them. There is a marriage discord that keeps the relationship shaky. The disgruntled partner feels like there is no way they can turn to. To fill that void in their heart, they seek solace in someone else's company.

Finally, some unfulfilled desires make one have an affair. 52% of partners, according to one research study, are dissatisfied with their sex lives. They lack intimacy and care from their partner. There is little interest that the partner shows in the physical act or keeps delaying or refusing. This can lead to frustration being built up inside, driving one to seek physical intimacy from outside the relationship. Partners who complain of their sex lives being unfulfilled think that they have every right to have the kind of intimacy they deserve. However, instead of discussing the core issues with their partner, they find it easier to just cheat.

Signs Your Partner Is Cheating On You

Strangely, the partner that has been cheated on begins to recognize all the signs they hadn't noticed before. They realize they were stupid to not be suspicious of the changes in their partner's habits, schedules, and behaviors. This happens. When you know your partner is loyal to you, you let go of many things. You don't pay attention because, in your mind, they are forever yours. You dismiss their anger as stress. You ignore their sudden need for dressing sharp, thinking they are doing so to impress their boss. You overlook how they have become cautious about what they eat because to you, it means they are finally taking up your advice on staying in shape. You act naïve and believe their stories when they turn up late or don't show up at all to important events.

Once you find evidence, all these instances where you had ignored and dismissed your negative thoughts about them, come back to you, laughing at you.

But why wait for them to act on their urges and not catch them before? Why not change their mind and intention about doing something they are going to regret later? Why not save yourself from being hurt? Here are a few signs that will tell you that your partner is planning on cheating on you or has already done it.

They Put More Effort To Look Good

From perfumes to clothes, and shoes, they have suddenly become cautious about the way they look. They spend more time looking at themselves in the mirror, trimming their beard, putting on cologne, and wearing contrasting cufflinks. They are worried about gaining weight and therefore, stressing about making healthy meals. Their hair looks different, they have started to spend more time at the gym, and pay more attention to their grooming. All these are classic signs that they are trying to impress someone. Chances are, they are having an affair and thinking about taking things forward.

They Are Home Less Often

Every other night has become a late-night from work. They are no longer excited to visit places with you, plan to dine outs, or go shopping. They show little interest in anything you say or want to do with them because they are always on their phone, messaging and taking calls. There are abrupt business meetings and trips for the weekend. If your partner is spending less time with you, chances are they are spending more time with someone else. Be vigilant about their whereabouts, ask them where they have been, and check out with their work friends if they are telling the truth. Chances are, someone will nudge and give you a sign that someone new has entered their life.

They Seem Interested In Knowing Your Plans For The Weekend

Suddenly, they want to know when you will be going out and when you will be back. They seem invested in your schedule and where you will be at a certain hour of the day. They are even keener about knowing when you will be back home. If you sense that your partner is overly interested in knowing your comings and goings, then know that they are looking for pockets of time to go meet someone else. They are just playing safe to not get caught.

They Have Become Possessive Of Their Things

Cheating partners have the habit of keeping their belongings to themselves. When they have an affair with someone, they don't like to share their items like phone, laptop, or car with you. When they catch you with their phone or laptop, they seem panicked and are quick to take them away. They may also take their phone with them in the shower when they didn't use it previously. This kind of possessiveness and obsession with their belongings suggests that there is something they are hiding.

They Experience An Increase Or Decrease In Libido

They are either too hungry for sex or not hungry at all. In most cases of infidelity, the partner having an affair loses interest in their spouse/significant other. Since they are getting it from someone else and because it seems more exciting, there is a decrease in their urges to have sex at home. However, if they are guilt-ridden, they might try to have more of it. They see it as a means to cover their tracks as well as feel that if they have increased intimacy with their partners, they might never find out about them cheating. If you notice any of these changes in their behavior, consider it a sign.

They Aren't Interested In Sharing Details About Their Day

Not long ago, there was a time when they wouldn't stop talking about their day from the minute they entered home. They would talk about their mean boss, their cunning colleague, and the new guy from the finance department that has the habit of poking his nose in the matters of others. They would tell you who they saw outside the office, where they stopped by for gas, and what they bought or ate during the day. They will then tell you how their workout session was at the gym, and how dreadful the traffic in the city was getting. But now, things have changed. Unless you ask them about their day, they rarely talk about it. They no longer share those intimate details. They tell you less because they are telling all these things to someone else now. They have found a new partner to share the intimate details of their day with.

They Accuse You Of Cheating

When partners cheat, they become hostile towards the other partner. To rationalize their behavior, they push the blame onto you and accuse you of cheating. They tell you that you no longer look at them the way you used to, aren't as affectionate as you were before, and certainly not adventurous in the bedroom anymore. They basically try to blame you for wanting to have some fun in life because you don't give it to them. They act as if nothing you do is right and therefore, you deserve to be cheated upon. Don't worry. They do make themselves feel better about what they are doing. But it is wrong on all levels. You aren't to blame.

They Change Their Schedule For No Reason

Partners having lived together for many years have predictable schedules. From home to office, office to gym, and then to the grocery store on the way back home...this is how it goes for most of them. However, if all of a sudden, they have been working late and have little to explain for themselves or their whereabouts, chances are, they are having an affair.

There Are Unexplained Expenses

There is suddenly a shortage of money in your partner's credit card, their bank statement shows a significantly decreased amount deposited. They are withdrawing the amount from their savings or retirement account. When you ask them where the money is going, they say they have invested it somewhere and you shouldn't worry about it. Infidelity is expensive. You buy gifts, dinners, wine, and trips for the one you are involved in. These costs, no matter how small, can add up pretty quickly. Therefore, if you notice any expensive purchases from places you rarely visit, chances are they are visiting them with someone else.

They Rarely Get Upset Anymore

If you think they are showing more patience than before about the things they used to get upset about instantly, it isn't a good sign. It might seem like one but it means they are least interested. If you used to have fights occasionally and suddenly they seem distant and focused elsewhere, it is another sign that they are focusing on their passions elsewhere. When partners find someone else, they seem less affected by the issues in their relationship. Their attention is engaged elsewhere, which is why it doesn't matter to them if you have burned their shirt while ironing anymore.

They Stop Envisioning The Future

Almost all couples, whether they have started dating or have been together for years have plans. They know what their goals are in the next five years and how they are going to achieve them. However, if your partner has found someone else, they may not be invested in the vision you two created, anymore. If they seem less interested in making new plans with you for the future, know that it's a sign that they are making them with someone else.

Can couples move past infidelity? This is a pressing question and unlike other issues, this one is more complicated. This isn't like lying. This isn't one with a controlling, insecure, or jealous partner. This is an issue where one partner has committed a crime, a heinous one. But move past infidelity is possible. Many couples do. Despite being caught, their partners forgive them and stay together. But there has to be a shared desire to do so. The partner shouldn't feel compelled to stay together because they have no family support, have kids to tend to, or are alone and dependable on their partner. They should stay because they want to. That being said, there is a lot of work that needs to be done here. A substantial amount of emotional, mental, and psychological work is needed to repair something that's broken. Most couples seek professional help when they want to live together but can't seem to get over the incident that is between them.

What Can You Do About It

Speaking from experience and after talking to many marriage counselors, there are three steps involved in moving past infidelity. But before we get to those, there is something important to note here. Infidelity or cheating doesn't only mean having sexual relations with someone. Cheating is a broad term that can include everything from secretly texting someone, staying in touch with an ex, wanting to sleep with someone, or doing so. There are many levels to it, with infidelity being the most gruesome of all.

Since we are looking at the breaking of the sacred bond by having sexual relations with someone other than the partner, the three-step method applies to this alone.

The first step involves identification and acknowledgment of the problem. As their partner, you have to come to terms with the fact that infidelity has been committed and there is no going back. What you can do is identify the causes that led to it. Go back to the many reasons and causes we discussed earlier and find out which one is it? Was there a lack of sexual desire? Did your partner feel unloved and unappreciated? Was there long-distance to blame? Was their emotional abandonment from your end to blame? Knowing the reasons can help you devise a plan to move forward and once again, fall in love.

Next, you must renegotiate the terms and conditions of the relationship. Seek a mutually agreed-upon resolution. Decide what role each of you has to play to make the relationship sustainable. What must you do to prevent it from happening again? Also, set consequences in place too. If it happens again, what will be the course of action? How will you respond to that? Have your reasons to stay and forgive them be clear and loud but also warn that they won't get another chance after this. Promise to work on the issues that led to cheating if they involve you and make a genuine effort to forgive.

Finally, commit to invest time, emotional work, and energy into the new resolutions. Stick to your side of the bargain and try your best to give your partner what they seek. For example, if they found you as a nagging and unappreciative partner, work on how you can be more appreciative and respectful towards them. Similarly, they should try to be more open and communicative about their needs instead of going behind your back and cheating.

Part Two

What Happens Next?

TRUST IS THE BELIEF you have in your partner that they won't break your heart. You trust them to take care of your well-being and happiness. You know that whatever they do, they have your best interest at heart. They live up to your expectations by staying true to their promises. Trust serves as the cornerstone for every healthy and prosperous relationship. It allows partners to be vulnerable with one another and feel safe.

When trust is missing, you are forced to worry about what they are doing, where they are, and who they are with. You feel threatened. You can't be sure that they will be there when you need them. You can't be vulnerable with them because you fear they will take advantage of you. You can't share your secrets with them because you are afraid they will disclose them to everyone. You can't form a deep connection with them because you don't feel ready to give all of yourself to them. When trust is broken, the relationship is a lot like quicksand. If the issues aren't remedied, it can mean the end of it.

Many couples have trouble with trust issues. Each has its own set of unique problems to handle. Because of the length of time, different personalities, and complexity of relationships, it is natural for one partner to feel betrayed by the other. In this age and time, it is hard to live up to one's expectations, especially when better options are just a click away, thanks to apps like Tinder, Bumble, OkCupid, etc.

But remember, all it takes is a single incident to break someone's trust that took yards to build.

Couples that stay together but fail to trust one another don't receive the benefits of being in a loving relationship. They keep fighting, arguing, accusing, and abusing one another emotionally. They don't reap benefits like improved health, a sense of joy, emotional well-being, and comfort. When you are with a partner who doesn't trust you, you can feel isolated, unwanted, and uncertain. They will forever doubt your actions, even loving gestures, leaving you disheartened and hurt. Without trust, a relationship is nothing more than a source of anxiety, frustration, and despair.

When trust is broken, you experience several emotions linked with betrayal. For instance, anger, which happens to be the most prominent one, is a result of feelings misread, misunderstood, and doubted. Suddenly, you have to prove all your actions so that your partner is convinced that you are trustworthy. This can cause you to feel angry towards your partner. Then, there is regret. Why did you trust them in the first place? It can be a painful realization that you put so much trust in them and they went on and broke it. You gave them such an important place in your heart, and yet, they betrayed your trust. The third is sadness, which is similar to regret. You feel sad because the relationship you two share isn't a healthy one. The foundation of it has been shattered with the breaking of trust. You feel unsure whether you can continue to live like this or should part ways. Next is fear, the fear of not knowing how you will react next, what you might say or so and cause more hurt.

All these thoughts urge you to question if the relationship is salvageable. Should you continue to put trust in them if they seem sorry? Should you stay and work to keep the relationship or are you stupid to do so? What if they take advantage of your empathy and consideration over and over again and then come begging for your forgiveness? If they already do so, for how long will this continue further? How will you get over the hurt and anger you feel towards them? Will you ever be able to cultivate feelings of love towards them?

The most important one being: can your relationship strive after trust has been broken?

The short answer to this is "Yes." Yes, the trust can be rebuilt but it is a challenging and complicated feat. You see, each relationship is different. So is every issue between couples. Depending on how much damage has been done, how much work will be needed, how the process of recovery will take place, and how long it will take to make it possible are all variables that differ from couple to couple. Some are quick to recover from the hurt while others need months of healing. For some, the damage isn't bigger than what they two share between them, and for some, it is too big to recover from. Some couples are willing to put in the work while others believe that they should part ways.

Rebuilding Trust = Behavior/Time

Has their behavior changed after they broke your trust? If yes, then it will take less time for you to recover because you can actually see them trying hard to save it. If their behavior remains the same and nothing seems to change, then it will take more time for you and your partner to recover from the hurt and move forward. They will need to be reminded of what they did and how it affected you. They will need to be taught how they can make things better and what changes they will have to bring into their actions and behaviors.

Just remember that it is going to be a mutual effort. You both will have to take an equal part in it. You both should be willing to try and resolve the issues that caused the breaking of trust in the first place and reassess your priorities. Additionally, you will have to be more open and expressive about your needs and how you want them to be addressed.

This section will focus on the signs of whether the relationship is worth saving or not. It will insist on giving your partner another chance but being smart and vigilant.

Is The Relationship Salvageable?

AGAIN, THIS COMES DOWN to looking at the damage that has been done. For example, if your partner broke your trust by lying to you or being too controlling and insecure, then there are many ways to address that. Similarly, if the trust was broken with incidents/several incidents of cheating, then it is another story. Even then, partners can recover and stay together. But the question is whether they should or not.

To ease this quest and understand the dynamics of the damage, below is a helpful guide to help you analyze where you and your partner stands and decide if the relationship is worth continuing or not.

The Thought Of Leaving Them Scares You

If you have ever dumped someone in life, you know that "I am done" feeling quite well. You know when it's time to pack your bags, get out of the door and leave. You don't look back because nothing is stopping you or holding you down. However, when you know something is worth saving, you walk back right in after you have packed your bags and walked out of the door. You come back because what's inside is more important than the reason for which you left. If you have found someone that the thought of ever leaving them scares you, know that the relationship is worth giving another shot. If you lay awake at night, wondering what life would look like without them if something were to happen to them, then stay and make things work. Some reasons prevent you from moving forward. So begin by focusing on the positives. Focus on what matters. Focus on what you can't live without. Recall the reasons that attracted them to you in the first place. Ask yourself why did you get in a relationship with them? Answering these questions should help you decide better.

You Feel Sad When You Think About Them Moving On

It isn't just jealousy or insecurity that stops you in your tracks from leaving them. If you genuinely can't accept the thought that after you break up, sooner or later, they will find someone else and be happy, then you need to rethink about leaving. Does the thought of them snuggle with someone else, paying anyone else the kind of attention they do to you makes you mad, then it is a sign that you aren't ready to let go just yet?

You Mention Breaking Up When Angry

Pretty sure every couple has done it once or twice when arguing with one another–accusing each other of regretting their decision to ever get in a relationship with you. However, if you only do it when you are hot with anger, it means that you only see your partner as ditch-worthy when you are angry. Those aren't your real thoughts. They are just there to help you feel less guilty and bad about yourself. When you say those words to someone, you want to hurt them in a place where it really hurts. You may not even mean them.

Your Fights Don't Escalate To A Point Where There Is No Going Back

When you are in a long-term relationship, you are aware of what ticks your partner, what actions would get them mad, what would make them fall more in love with you, what would hurt them the most etc. You are no stranger to one another's fears and insecurities. When you both fight, you can unleash some true meanness. But you don't. You stay within the limits and tone down when things start to get out of hand. You both know at what point one should back down and call it a day. You don't let your fights escalate to a point where real nasty stuff gets out. You always stop yourself from stooping low and hurting them. This shows that you still care about one another and have respect for each other's feelings. This is worth saving.

You Are Sure The Sparks Can Be Rekindled

You still feel love towards one another and are sure that if you work hard enough, you can still have the kind of relationship that you had before they broke your trust. Despite all the fighting and arguing that goes on, there is still some chemistry between you two. You two still laugh at each other's jokes, not each other like no one else does, and are aware of each other's vulnerabilities too well. You know that with some healing, you can be back at infusing back excitement in your relationship.

You Are Vulnerable With One Another

In today's age and time, it is hard to open up with someone and trust them fully to keep all your secrets safe. If you can confide in your partner about your deepest, darkest, and twisted secrets without an ounce of guilt or shame, know that the relationship is worth saving. You don't find people as such every day. If you can confidently share your flaws, fears, and secrets with them, you can talk to them about what happened and why it happened too, and get over it.

You Still Care For One Another

Apart from mistrust, if you two still care about one another, their well-being, and happiness, then the relationship is worth salvaging. If they get on your nerves and you still want to wake up beside them the next morning, then it means they are too precious to lose.

There's No One Like Them

You have had your share of past boyfriends and there is a reason why you chose to be with them. You chose to stay even when you stopped seeing eye to eye on things because you knew they were worth it. You chose to stay because their positives outweigh their negative qualities. There are so many things that you adore about them as opposed to the ones you despise. There has never been anyone like them and you are sure no one will be. They are perfect for you in many ways, and therefore, you are forced to consider whether you should stay back or leave. Stay and make things work. If they are perfect in every way and they feel the same about you, then surely you can find a way to reconcile and not lose each other.

You Have Been Through A Lot Together

Have you two been together through some tough times? Did your relationship stay strong despite those difficult times? Did it survive because you two were sure of each other? Maybe you can work this out too. Having a shared history and values is a hard match. If you have overcome financial, emotional, or physical hurdles together, then you might want to give this another try. After all, shared history also means many unforgettable memories. You can't create them with someone else.

Things Are Improving From Their End

Have they been extra careful, loving, and loyal? Do you see them making an effort to rebuild what was once broken? Are they putting in the work to improve their attitude and behavior towards yourself? If you think they are genuinely working to better themselves, then take a step back and ask yourself if they are worth giving up on. Maybe you can stay in for a little longer and see if you like this improved version of them or not. Maybe you can put them to the test and see for how long they continue to make the promised efforts? Do they forget all of it when there is a disagreement or do they try to understand your point of view?

AM I BEING STUPID OR SMART?

IF YOU STILL HAVEN'T figured it out yet and feel stupid for not knowing what your heart wants, maybe what you need is more time and a few more signs. Now, these signs put forth in the form of questions, mentioned below are based solely on their actions and behaviors and not yours. The first section talked about how you felt about them still. This next section deals with how they treat you and what efforts they are making, if any, to reinstall the lost trust.

Has It Become A Pattern?
Have they been making the same mistakes over and over again? Is this the fifth time they are asking you to reconsider, promising you that things will be different this time? Do they always break your trust purposely because they know you will forgive them?

If yes, then this has become more of a habit. If they keep doing something that they know upset you in the past, this is a pattern. It seems like they know that they will be forgiven regardless and thereof, keep taking advantage of your kindness. Don't forgive them this time. If they wanted to make things right and change, they would have done it the second time around. If they still repeat the same actions that caused you to hurt in the past and seem to be not getting the point, then it is better to leave and move on than stay and keep getting hurt. They aren't going to change and nothing you can do will change their attitude either. You deserve better than that!

Have They Accepted Their Mistake?

Sometimes, partners don't view their actions as mistakes or faults. They don't acknowledge that they have hurt you and put the blame on you for being too sensitive. If this is the case, you know what you need to do next. Run for the hills!

For any relationship to prosper successfully, both partners must admit when they were wrong and apologize. The first step is, however, acceptance of being wrong. If they show no regret whatsoever and think that you are being overdramatic, it might be a good call to just leave.

Have They Apologized Sincerely?

If they seem remorseful and know that they have messed up big time, then perhaps, you might want to rethink your decision. You won't be considered stupid if you decide to stay because they seem genuine. They could have just gaslighted you or dismissed your feelings but they didn't. Instead, they are making every effort to take the blame and apologize. It shows that they are sorry for how they behaved and caused you hurt. However, don't rush into accepting the apology. Take your time. Let them show it from their behavior how sorry they are. Once you accept their apology, you will be bound to stay. They will also see it as an opportunity to keep hurting you in the future if you rush it. You want them to think about what they have done and see how they have made you feel.

Will Getting Back Together Work?

Will you be able to make it through this together? Even if your partner messed up and you gave them another chance, it doesn't mean that it will only be them doing all the work alone. You will have to put in an effort too. You are an essential part of the relationship too. If you can't see yourself doing half the work and rebuilding the relationship from scratch, being more communicative about how you feel, and having difficult conversations when they are needed, then things might not work out between you two.

Are You Two Committed To Growing Together?

Are you both committed to growing as a couple together as well as individually? If yes, then this is a relationship worth investing in. If you two are willing to make the effort and work through the issues, determining what worked and what didn't and why, then you can successfully implement positive changes and make the relationship one that you both wanted.

Are Your Core Values The Same?

Do you have the same values? Is there a long-term vision that you two thrive for? Do you have the same interests, philosophy, and beliefs? It is very hard to come across someone that has the combo and if you are lucky enough to have found your soulmate, then perhaps you should think wisely about separation.

Does He Respect You?

To truly know if your relationship is worth saving or not is by knowing if they respect you and your feelings. Does he show a willingness to respect your feelings and how you think? Compatibility doesn't require that you two are always on the same page. Even your differences can keep things exciting and balanced. But any relationship requires mutual respect and honor for how one thinks and feels. If they show respect towards that, then forgive them.

Are Your Expectations Realistic?

Do you have realistic expectations of your partner? Just because they messed up doesn't make you the alpha in the relationship. You don't negate its terms alone. You can set some boundaries and rules if you decide to take them back but setting unrealistic expectations even though you know they can't meet, is wrong. No one is perfect. If they have apologized and shown remorse for what they did, it should be enough. Don't set expectations so high that they fail to meet them and disappoint you once again. There will be times when they will make mistakes again, so go in with a realistic viewpoint.

Every relationship has its ups and downs. Every couple has its differences. Shared goals and values, how you feel around them, and what feelings they enliven within you, are all signs that suggest a good relationship. Just know that if they seem truly apologetic and remorseful, if you are willing to forgive and move forward, you can end up with a stronger relationship than before.

But I Am Still Hurt And Angry

HAVING LEARNED ABOUT THE signs and questions, you may have a fairly clear idea of what you want. Do you want to stay and work on the relationship or let your partner go and move on? If you decide to stay and work on the wrong things, you must still be very angry and hurt with your partner.

Forgiveness must be the last thing on your mind because you feel betrayed. You feel taken advantage of. You feel like you have been tossed aside and left to rot. How could they be forgiven for what they did?

Experiencing these feelings in the initial days is a normal reaction. Your grief is bigger than their apology. You feel it is not enough to just say sorry and seem guilty. You want more. You expect more. However, as days pass by and you begin to heal, you realize that maybe forgiveness isn't that hard after all, provided that they are making a genuine effort to make things work.

Forgiveness involves giving up the right to further punish your spouse for what they did or didn't do. It is about letting that bitterness fester no more. It is about letting them know that you are done grieving over what happened and ready to talk about the next steps. So you have to be extremely careful because once you tell them that you have forgiven them, you can no longer bring up things from the past and use them as a weapon to get them to do your bidding. You can't shame them over and over again or remind them of what happened. You have to be careful and ready mentally and emotionally to let go of the grudge that you hold against them and move forward.

Remember, it isn't the snakebite that kills one, it is the venom. You can't un-bite yourself once it has happened. The bite isn't the reason that causes death. You get bitten by a mosquito, a bee, or any other animal like a bird or cat and survive. What makes snakebite lethal and poisonous is the venom it contains.

Putting that into context, the snakebite is the situation that happened to you. The venom, however, is the negative feelings and thoughts that come along with it. Luckily, there are many ways to prevent the venom from getting into your veins and corrupting them with its poison. Similarly, you have the chance to either prevent negative thoughts from corrupting your mind or let them run free through your veins. As long as the feelings remain free and undealt with, they will poison the mind slowly and then all at once. Then there is no going back from that point.

In this example, forgiveness is anti-venom. It is both the healer and the cure. It is the first mode of prevention from stopping the venom from taking over your mind. You may have difficulties dealing with the pain but forgiveness will set you free. If you choose to forgive, it is only a matter of time before the healing starts to happen.

A lot of people assume that forgiveness means condoning your partner's actions. It doesn't. It doesn't mean that you are surrendering yourself to your feelings. It means you are setting them free. Forgiveness means that you choose to carry the pain no longer. You allow yourself to be free of those negative thoughts and emotions about your partner and be at a place of peace and be free.

Coming to how to truly forgive and forget your partner for breaking your trust, here are some key points you must keep in your mind, moving forward.

Let Go Of Your Anger Towards Them

They made a mistake and apologized. Don't hold it against them anymore. Show respect and affection towards them as you did before. Don't lash out at them because they did something to mildly hurt or offend you.

Don't Punish Or Sulk

Don't think about trying to fix them. Don't make them feel isolated by pushing them away. Don't do things like not talking to them the whole day just to prove why they shouldn't do the same to you ever again. It will only make them feel more guilty and perhaps, even angry. Instead, try to resolve the situation.

Show Empathy

If there is a possibility that what they didn't wasn't intentional, show empathy. Try to put yourself in their shoes and see their reasons for hurting you. What if you had done the same? What if you had committed the same mistake? Doing so will allow you to view things from their perspective without judgment.

Drop The Tough Act

If you think that forgiving them and going back to how things were will make you come off as weak or vulnerable, you are wrong. There is no power-play here. You two are human beings who happen to be in love. Don't let your anger come in the way of your relationship. Drop the act where you pretend to be harsh towards them.

Don't Keep Score

Again, you are a couple. You have to resolve your issues as a team. There is no point in keeping score and thinking that I am going to let this slide so that when I make a mistake, I can expect the same behavior. You aren't up against each other. How about treating one another with love and care rather than with hate and envy? Use this opportunity to spread positivity, not negativity.

Look At What Triggered Their Actions

What made them commit a crime so hurtful that it left you wounded? Could you have pushed their buttons too far? Could your actions or lack of actions cause them to go elsewhere and seek the respect, love, and appreciation they deserve?

Deal With One Issue At A Time

Every time there is an argument between you two, you will be tempted to pull out the guilt card. You know this is one thing that would end the conversation. Remember, doing so will only cause hurt and even intensify the conflict between you two. It will lead to deepening the divide between you two. Therefore, try to pick one issue at a time and deal with it first. Then move on to another and get it done with. You can easily get overwhelmed when you try to handle more than you can, at once.

Now that you have decided to forgive them, be clear about your perspective. Sit down and give each other uninterrupted time to discuss and share your concerns. If you happen to notice that you are just trading barbs back and forth, not much hearing will happen. You both will be busy accusing one another and making matters worse. Take your time to express your concerns, emotions, and behaviors. Give them the same opportunity to share with you their grievances towards you. Once you two have your perspectives communicated, you can come up with a mutual strategy to move forth.

Part Three

The Preventive Measures Checklist

BUILDING TRUST IS A complex word of webs and promises that are fragile. All it takes is one incident to break trust. Even if it took you a lifetime of devotion, care, and affection to build it, it can be broken with a few lies, cheating, or wrongdoing. But what if there were some ways we could prevent the trust from breaking? What if we could learn to not let mistrust sabotage our relationships before we start one? Some easy-to-miss actions and behaviors lead to the breaking of trust. Many of us are not even aware of committing these mistakes because they rarely get pointed out by our friends and family. However, when a partner enters your life and you share it with them, things begin to change. These habits and actions become questionable as they have a direct impact on the person you are living with. For example, something as simple as not calling/texting your partner when you are running late can become a debatable issue with a partner. They have a right to know if you have made other plans on the way and will be late. It is a responsible and mature thing to do. Your friends might have not cared enough to call or text back to know where you were but your partner might. This isn't them being in the wrong, it is you. Not knowing where you are and what you are doing can lead to all sorts of negative thoughts in your partner's mind. If this is becoming a routine, they might become suspicious of your actions and if you fail to give them a satisfactory answer, it can break their trust.

Therefore, this next section is dedicated to working on yourself to ensure that you don't end up breaking your partner's trust in you. It is aimed at letting you know the importance of healthy dialogue, honesty, and openness in relationships whilst highlighting the behaviors and actions that promote mistrust.

Putting In The Work From The Get-Go

THIS IS PIVOTAL. IT doesn't matter if you have just gotten into a relationship or are preparing yourself to get into one, the first step involves working on yourself so that you can avoid the mistakes other people make. For instance, you must know what you want out of the relationship. You must know what your demands and needs are and how a partner will address them.

Similarly, you must know what qualities you want to see in a potential partner, particularly ones that you don't have or would like to have someday. If you are too panicky, you might want a partner that remains calm and knows how to carry themselves in tough situations. Who knows their calmness rubs off on you and improves the way you handle situations in your life. Likewise, if you are too easy-going, you may seek someone with the same attitude so that they don't become too dependable on you. If you don't do well with instructions and dictation, you may want to partner with someone that is composed and non-controlling. This is how you must begin your search for the right partner.

The qualities you need to build and work on upon yourself include building self-confidence and self-worth. At all times, you must know that you don't have to bow to anyone out of love or fear. You are a unique individual and shouldn't have to compromise on your values and beliefs. You shouldn't have to change for a partner because they want you to. You should bring positive change in yourself on your terms. Partners that lack self-esteem and self-confidence forever remain unsure of themselves. They think they don't deserve what they have and consider themselves lucky. This can end with them being taken advantage of, for their naivety and simplicity. They can easily be manipulated because they cherish what they have and will want to continue with the relationship no matter what. You don't want to be like them. You have to be clear about what you want and what you deserve.

Finally, you must make yourself trustworthy. Your partner should feel like they can count on you for everything they need. They should know that you are being honest and transparent. They should feel like they are with someone they can rely on and trust with their secrets. They shouldn't have to doubt your actions or intentions because your behavior seems fishy. Being trustworthy in a relationship is one of the most basic needs. Without trust, there can't be a healthy relationship. If you expect your partner to be honest, transparent, and trustworthy, set an example by being all these things yourself.

Actions That Violate Trust

SPEAKING OF THE ACTIONS and habits that break the trust between married couples and partners, we have the following. Note how simple and easy-to-forget these habits and actions are. If you find yourself doing any of these with a potential partner, know that you are digging a ditch for yourself. If they can't trust you, they won't stay with you. If you want a fulfilling relationship, don't do these as these actions violate a partner's trust.

Exclusion

If you are at a party or family gathering with your plus-one, don't exclude them from the group or conversation. If they have agreed to come along and be a part of what seems to be an important event to you, it is your job to ensure that they have a good time. Don't make private jokes where they don't seem to get the context or talk about things they have no idea of. These subtle actions convey to them that they aren't needed.

Keeping Secrets From Them

Understandably, you don't want to be openly vulnerable with them if you have just started dating. However, if several months have passed and you still have kept big secrets about yourself or your family or job from them, then it is wrong. Being secretive with a spouse or partner is never advised. It can be annoying to find out something major about you from someone else. Similarly, if you don't let them touch your phone or have passwords on all your gadgets, they may start to wonder if there is something you are hiding from them. This can lead to baseless suspicion, which is why it is best to come clean about things and be open and transparent with them.

Being Jealous

If you hate the idea of them spending time with anyone but you, then you need to work on yourself. You can't expect them to cling to you for everything. They have a life of their own and friends that they would like to hang out with. Expecting them to spend all their free time with you and feeling jealous when they don't, is going to push them away from you. No one needs that kind of a person in their lives. Acting jealous will lead them to think that they aren't trustworthy and offend them.

Stalking

Keeping tabs on where they are, who they are with, or what they are doing, is another thing you need to work upon before getting into a serious relationship. Stalking your partner on social media, via tracking apps, and following them in your car will go south when they come to know of it. Your intentions might be pure but they might not see it like that. Therefore, show some trust in their judgment and decisions. Let them live their life without being monitored 24/7.

Remaining Emotionally Unavailable

It is one of the requisites of any solid relationship to be able to tell your partner anything and everything. However, if you keep to yourself and don't express how you feel, how can you expect them to take the hint? If there is a lack of communication on your part, it will end with frustration for both of you. Your partner will feel like you aren't in the relationship fully whereas you would think that your partner isn't making an effort to get to know you. Similarly, they need to know how you feel about them now and then. They need to know if they are still loved and adored the same way. Not letting them in on your feelings towards them can make them feel alone and unwanted.

Lying

Lying to your partner about the simplest of things just to keep up a rapport is a guaranteed deal-breaker. You shouldn't have to hide your flaws from them and mask them with lies. They deserve to be with a partner that is honest and transparent. Don't try to hide things or lie. If you are caught, it will be hard for them to trust you again.

Cheating

Cheating has more to do with just hooking up with someone. Casual flirting, staying in touch with an ex, or acting all dreamy about TV stars and celebrities also counts as subtle cheating. Your partner should deserve all the praise and attention there is. How would you feel if your partner kept looking at other females with lust in their hearts? Now imagine what you put through your partner.

Keeping Important Details From Them
Sometimes, we feel it is okay to hide or obscure some facts of a story from our partners. We deliberately drop them out, thinking they aren't that important. However, a deliberate attempt means you don't want them finding out about it on purpose. If you are telling them something, then they deserve a full disclosure, not just half of the story. If they find it out by someone else, it can erode their trust in you.

TRAITS THAT MAKE YOU APPEAR UNTRUSTWORTHY

APART FROM YOUR ACTIONS, there are some traits and qualities that don't sit well with a potential partner. Since we are on the subject of preventing breaking of trust, we must cover every aspect that can ruin your chances of finding your soulmate. This next section covers some of the traits that many of us have that come off as fishy or untrustworthy.

Unpunctuality

Any potential partner wants to be with someone they can rely on. This is what establishes trust in the first place. If you keep falling back on your promises, don't show up when you promised to, or are always caught up in other things, it can sabotage your relationship. It can make them seem unimportant and make it harder for them to rely on you. Being on time, showing that you care, and trying your best to make an effort to be there for them, instills trust. Although a small request, this can really mean a lot to a partner that values time and wants to be able to trust you.

Judgmental Nature

If you have the habit of being judgmental, it too can sabotage your relationship. It's hard to confide in judgmental people. As a partner, you want to be open with them and share your stuff. However, if they keep judging everything you say, or worse, belittle or demean your journey and past, you can feel like you are on a pedestal in front of a judge. You don't want that kind of a partner and your partner doesn't deserve one like that, either. As your partner, they shouldn't feat your judgment. They shouldn't have to withhold things from you or rely on their friends to vent out. They should feel free to come to you.

Poor Listener

Your partner deserves an observant and dedicated listener. They want someone that can read between the lines, guess their inner state by the way they look, body language, and facial expressions. They want someone who would listen without judgment and refrain from offering unsolicited advice unless asked to. They want someone to whom they can come home to, tell how their day was, and feel relieved and happy to have a partner that acknowledges all that they do. If you are a poor listener, start to offer advice and suggestions without even listening to them, fail to notice their current state, and disregard their emotions casually, you are not the right fit for them. Work on how to become an effective communicator as well as an effective listener so that your partner feels loved and listened to. Show that you are invested in what they have to say. That would make you more trustworthy.

Hatred Towards Their Family And Friends

How would you feel if your partner always makes up excuses to ditch a family event or a social get-together with your friends? Would you not feel offended that they don't make an effort to like them and support you? Now reverse the situation and imagine how they feel when you keep showing hatred towards their loved ones. Some people in your partner's life are going to be there forever. You can't decide who they remain friends with or not. However, bringing it up repeatedly and expecting them to ditch their friends for you, isn't a justifiable request? It can breed negativity in the relationship and make you come off as less trustworthy.

Irresponsibility

When it comes to doing your part, your partner can't rely on you. When you are asked to do something, you make up excuses to avoid doing it or delay it until the last minute. Sometimes, it is your partner that ends up doing it after all. This may not seem like an issue because partners are supposed to help each other out, but it is becoming a routine, it can turn off your partner. As their other half, they expect you to do your part of the chores and if you fail to be responsible about them, it just shows a lack of investment. You have to hold up to your end of the bargain or revisit the house rules once again. When you fail to act responsibly, it puts additional pressure on your partner. They can't always have your back and some days, they wish that you would act like an adult. It can leave your partner thinking that you aren't ready for serious commitment aka marriage and kids because you can't seem to take care of a pet or the house.

Being Honest, Transparent, and Open To Dialogues

MOST IMPORTANTLY, HONESTY IS important in relationships, all types of them. Whether new or old, honesty is one of those things that keeps the relationship intact. It is what trust is based on. Intuitively, we all know that it's a good thing. Most of the time, we try to put it into practice too. However, sometimes, we feel like we will be misunderstood by our partners and therefore, lie. No matter how rocky your relationship is, your partner doesn't deserve to be lied to. If there are lies involved, it means that communication between you two isn't healthy. If you have to keep things from your partner, fearing their reaction, then you two need to sit down and express how you feel.

When we say honesty is important in your relationship, what do I actually mean?

Honesty in relationships means always speaking the truth. It means being authentic, transparent with our words, and straightforward with our actions. It means never lying, hiding the truth, or purposely misdirecting or omitting the truth from the people you care about.

Honesty with a partner means that you tell them the truth and be open about both big and small things in your life. If you feel like you have to avoid telling your partner something, perhaps something that bothers you in the relationship, then it means you aren't being honest with them. Similarly, if you feel like you have to keep something from them because you know it will make them upset, then you aren't being honest. If you think that by omitting or misdirecting the truth, you are saving them from hurt, then you aren't being an honest partner.

If you are with them, they shouldn't have to worry about being bothered, upset, or hurt.

Being honest in a relationship means that you are your most authentic self when around your partner. It means that you don't have to suppress your emotions or feelings because you fear rejection or being ridiculed. If you feel like you have to hide your true personality from them, then you need to rethink your relationship.

As stated earlier, being honest with your partner cultivates a safe space for you and your partner. You can both communicate in healthy ways and resolve issues without letting them fester for long. Couples should be able to talk about anything and everything with their partners without being judged or humiliated. They should be able to be real with one another and form a strong connection. Being honest means that you will be proactive about acknowledging and addressing any issues, tension, or conflicts that arise in the relationship, and confidently bring them up. Relationships flourish when partners can meet one another on the same level. Relationships flounder when they can't trust each other's words and intentions behind those words and actions.

Believe it or not, you can't hide being impenetrable for long. You may think that you have successfully hidden a fact from your partner but sooner or later they are going to find out. Remember how in part one, we discussed the various signs and trademarks of liars? They make up stories to cover up for their lies and are inconsistent with them, making their partner more and more suspicious. When you choose dishonesty, you rob your partner or spouse of the opportunity to love the real you. Honesty, transparency, and open communication between partners encourage growth. It adds depth to relationships. It builds a strong foundation, establishing trust. It makes partners feel like they are on the same team rather than opposed to each other.

Moreover, we aren't meant to be by ourselves. Humans are social animals, after all. We rely on one another to fulfill our needs. It is the "give and take" that makes life more meaningful. Not being honest in a relationship is like planting a pit for yourself. Eventually, you will find yourself in it. When you rely on another person for your happiness, sadness, and every other accompanying need, you have to be honest with them. You rely on their support and guidance and when you offer it, it should feel genuine. So how can you be more honest, transparent, and open to communicate with your partner? Below are a few ideas.

Be Consistent

Stick to your promises. Do what you say you will do so that your partner knows that they can rely on you for anything. To build trust, you don't just need big words. You need to show it through your actions too. For example, if you promised that you will spend more time with them over the weekend because you couldn't the previous week, don't make any other plans. Nothing builds resentment and erodes trust like empty promises.

If you can't commit to doing the things you promised, don't make promises the next time. No one likes to be stood up. Your partner deserves the same level of respect as you do. If you promised to do something, they cleared their schedule for it too. So a broken apology won't do. The easiest way to avoid resentment is to not promise the things you can't do.

Make Open Communication Your Top Priority

Set aside a time every night to converse with one another. Talk about how your day went, talk about your plans, what things need work, plans for tomorrow or the weekend, etc., the more communicative you are, the fewer disagreements there will be. If something bothers you about your partner's actions or behavior, how else would they know to stop if you don't tell them?

Avoid Judgmental Remarks

When a partner opens up to you about something valuable and closest to their heart, keep your judgments to yourself and just listen with consideration and care. If you keep interrupting or disregarding how they feel, they will shut down emotionally. Even if they come to you to talk about a mistake they made, remain calm. Don't yell or use harsh words. Chances are, it will drive them away, and they will be less likely to remain honest in the future.

Part Four

Let's Fall In Love Again

THIS FINAL PART OF the book is all about putting into practice all that we have learned so far. Although there is no magical formula to do so, there are, however, some exercises and activities for couples to try out to find their way back to each other after trust has been broken. Many would want to leave and find someone else. But it takes courage and guts to stay and deal with what needs dealing. If you are one of those couples who want to work through the misunderstandings and heartbreak and want to give yourself another chance to rebuild trust, this section is for you. If you are willing to put in the work, I have some of the best, highly recommended by marriage counselors, activities, and exercises to apply the knowledge we now have.

The first three exercises discussed are for couples that want to establish a strong bond from the get-go. They want to develop trust and understanding by getting to know one another better. They are aimed at making you a better partner for any potential partner. If you become the ideal partner, you won't have trouble seeking one.

The final five are aimed at helping couples rebuild trust and work on themselves as a couple for improved intimacy, better understanding, and a deeper connection with one another.

The Naikan Reflection

The Naikan Reflection is a Japanese exercise designed for individuals to self-reflect and is reminded that they mustn't take their partner for granted. It focuses on the give and take in relationships. It is a simple exercise that takes no more than five minutes. Here's how you can start with it:

- Find a comfortable and distraction-free space, to begin with. Set aside your phone and any other distracting object in your path.

- Next, reflect on the past 24 hours of your life and recall the following with your partner in your mind.

- What have I given? This is where you make a list of all the things you did for your partner in the last 24 hours. Account for even the most minor things like bringing them the towel when they were in the washroom.

- What have I received? Now, make a mental list of all the things your partner did for you in the past 24 hours. Again, think about the smallest of gestures that go unnoticed most of the time like saving you some space on the couch, opening the door for you, taking out the groceries from the cat, etc.

- What troubles have I caused? Now envision all your actions that may have hurt your partner during those last 24 hours.

- Notice the emotions that arise. Do you feel positive about your actions or negative about them?

The exercise allows the practitioner to reflect on their actions and also on their partner's. Sometimes, we become so self-centered that we focus solely on ourselves and what we bring to the relationship. This exercise helps us realize the things that our partner does for us and as a result, we become more aware and attentive of their needs.

Extended Cuddle Time

According to a research report , increased cuddle time between couples lowers resting blood pressure and improves their sleeping patterns. This means that if you want to feel fuzzy, warm, and loved, just snuggle together for an extended time every night. The exercise is rather simple and achievable for every new and old couple.

The instructions simply involve pulling your partner closer to yourself in bed and cuddling them for as long as you like.

Cuddling proves to be a more effective and better way to end your day instead of looking at your tablets and phones. Science proves that the chemicals that are released during a hug improve mood, sleep, and deepen the connection. The exercise is to be practiced every night before bed or any other time that the couple finds suitable. The important thing is to have some one-on-one time to show affection and increase intimacy. To amplify its effect, you can even play some music in the background to promote positive thoughts and feelings.

Disclosure

Sharing secrets has always been a desirable and exciting exercise. You have been doing it since birth with your friends, parents, and siblings. At any age, knowing that someone entrusts you with a secret can be quite powerful. Why? It is because you don't share your deepest secrets, wishes, dreams, and desires with just anybody. They have to be special enough. They must have proved themselves worthy of it. It is hard to open up to just anybody because there is a chance that we will be ridiculed, judged, or misunderstood. However, when you do it with someone you are close to, it makes them feel special and important.

Sharing a secret, disclosing a past transgression, or admitting a mistake takes guts. It happens when you trust someone and know that they shall not break it. This next exercise is aimed at establishing trust between partners. Here's how to begin:

- You and your partner must find a safe and distraction-free space to begin with.

- Each of you must take turns disclosing a secret or embarrassing fact about yourself.

- The other must listen with concentration and not interrupt. They should hold their initial thoughts and reactions to it unless the other partner asks them to share them.

- Both partners take turns disclosing and listening to one another.

The reason this works so well is that it can help partners discuss issues and tensions between them and resolve them in a calm and relaxed manner. There is no yelling, name-calling, or verbal abuse involved. Both partners feel like they are in a safe environment and unburden their hearts. This will help them prevent the building up of frustration and negativity within them. It can make them more empathetic towards each other's needs.

Eye Gazing

Also referred to as soul searching, this is a popular couple exercise focusing on improving the connection between partners. Some studies suggest that long-held eye contact with a partner can help recognize many emotions, increase intimacy, and build trust. Eye gazing reduces boundaries between partners and they can both feel united. Besides, as Shakespeare puts it, the eyes are the window to the soul. How about giving it a try?

All you need is some basic instruction to begin.

• Start with facing your partner in either a seated or standing position. You two should be close enough to feel each other's breath on your face.

• Now, look into each other's eyes. Maintain eye contact for up to five minutes (minimum three minutes). You are allowed to blink as many times as you want.

• It may feel awkward at first but let the silence between you two become pleasant and familiar.

• If you have a hard time focusing on one another or maintaining eye contact, play a song in the background and let go once it ends.

This is an intense exercise that helps you connect with your partner better. It makes you see them for what they are, as eyes rarely tell lies. Your reflection in their eyes allows you to see how they view you and feel about you, thanks to the spark in them.

The 6-Second Kiss

This next exercise comes recommended by Dr. John Gottman, the renowned author and founder of the Gottman Institute. He suggests that kissing your partner for exactly six-second not only adds a dash of romance to an otherwise boring day but also releases the feel-good hormones that improve one's mood. The kiss is timed because six seconds is long enough to be intimate with a partner and become distracted from the busyness of the day.

Partners that feel there is a poor connection between them lately or want to work on improving intimacy can try the six-second kissing exercise to turn on the mood. Catch them in a distracted moment and have all their attention or do it first thing in the morning to set the mood right.

Icebreakers

This has been the most faithful of activities to bring people together. Icebreaker exercises are encouraged not only in relationships but also at schools, workplaces, and events to make everyone feel comfortable with one another and feel energized. When we apply the same technique to romantic relationships, we see it working wonders to improve conversation and trust among partners. This exercise comes with a set of questions that you and your partner would like to ask one another but rarely get the time to. This is where you get to know them a little better, even when you have known them for years. You will be astonished when you come across a fact or two that you never knew about your partner before now.

It is also a great way to get to those unresolved issues and set a time and date to work on them.

As stated, this comes with a list of questions that the partners can mutually agree upon. Some examples include:

- Tell me a childhood memory you can't forget.
- Tell me about an incident that changed your life.
- Tell me about your biggest fears.
- Tell me your favorite song and what it speaks to you.
- Tell me about someone that inspires you.
- Tell me about something that you love the most about our relationship.
- Tell me about something you would like to change about us/me.

This simple exercise can allow you two to become more connected and intimate with one another. You two can share secrets you never shared with anyone and feel more bonded.

- Start with scheduling a time for this. It could be an hour on a weekend or a weeknight.
- Prepare a list of questions on a sheet of paper or get hold of a Questions Workbook for couple.
- Let go of anything else you were engaged in before beginning.
- Take turns to ask each other one question from the list. You can have two separate lists or just one, depending on how

much time you have.

- Note down the topics that you want to discuss more, later.

Create a Wish-List

This is similar to the icebreaker exercise we talked about. A wish list, however, deals with more intimate and private questions that the couples want to discuss with one another. As the name suggests, the wish list accumulates wishes that you want your partner to know about.

- Start with taking out the time to create a personal wish list individually.

- Write down the things you wished your partner knew about you or the things you would like more/less of in the relationship.

- When creating the list, ensure that you use statements starting with "I" instead of "You," because you don't want to sound accusatory. For example, you can have a wish that reads something like this: "I wish you would help around the house more as I get tired tending to all the chores alone or," "I wish you would be more appreciative of the things I do because I feel unwanted and unloved most of the time."

- Once you have a wish list created, take turns sharing.

- Each partner should take turns to speak about a wish and then you two either acknowledge or mark it for further discussion.

- In the end, summarize what you two have heard.

- Lastly, describe to your partner how you would feel if your wishes come true. Be as expressive and elaborative as you can so your partner knows how desperately you want your wishes to come true.

The reason this exercise works so well is that all relationships have the potential to grow and become stronger than before. However, many wishes and desires remain unheard because we think they will initiate arguments and disagreements. So we keep them to ourselves. This exercise can prevent their suppression and let your partner become aware of them in the most relaxed way.

Relinquishing Control

In most relationships, there is an alpha and a beta. The alpha is the more dominant partner in the relationship and most commonly, the male. He is the one taking all the big initiatives like planning a vacation, deciding on what places are worth going on, and how family finances will be handled. Men are more dominant because of their personality traits and characteristics. The female simply controls what she is being told. Although this works for most couples, this type of dominance can lead to trust issues between partners where one feels burdened with having to decide all things and the other feels like they have no control over their lives.

It is time to switch things up and let couples experience what it is like to be in each other's shoes for once.

As the name of the exercise suggests, both partners switch roles and are left with the task of deciding and planning, and initiating. The other is tasked to accept and go with the suggested ideas.

- To perform the exercise, the dominant partner must relinquish control and give the partner a chance to step up and follow through. It can be anything from hosting a party at home or planning a trip together for the weekend.

- The dominant partner must verbalize and outline their expectations.
- The other partner must note them down and come up with a plan of action in a day.
- If the partner is successful with the task, we can conclude that they can be trusted.

This exercise allows both partners to experience what difficulties arise when they are in control or without it. Having experienced both ends of the spectrum, the partners can acknowledge and appreciate each other's roles in making things happen. It allows them to grow as a partner. The dominant partner learns what it is like to surrender control and be vulnerable whereas the other partner learns how to step up and take charge when it's needed. It makes them more reliable and consistent with what they do.

Conclusion

THE IMPORTANCE OF TRUST among partners, whether dating, married, or divorced, is an unarguable need. It is equally important for both new and established relationships. Lack of trust suggests an inability of both partners to connect with one another on a deep level. No relationship can thrive if there is no room for a deeper connection. There is always something new and exciting you can learn about your partner if there is trust between you two.

Abuse of trust in romantic relationships is the perfect recipe for disasters. Couples that violate each other's trust can never have what is called a healthy and happy relationship. Their minds are clouded with doubts and suspicions about their partner. They can never know if they are being honest, controlling, or secure. There is always that gut feeling to recheck and reassure things. This isn't ideal for your emotional or mental health. As a partner, you should be able to trust their words, actions, and behaviors. You should have complete faith in them to not lie, cheat, or betray you. You should feel safe with them. You should feel unpressurized and free to be yourself.

A lot of times, partners fail to realize the harm their words and actions cause. They are unaware of how their partner feels. This usually happens when there are suppressed negative emotions. Partners feel incapable of expressing their desires and communicating their needs. But the expression of one's desires, needs, and wishes are what helps couples grow as a team. However, this is impossible if there is a lack of trust between them.

This is where the activities and exercises come into play, discussed in part four of the book. They are aimed at helping you communicate with your partner in an open and expressive manner as well as focus on your own shortcomings along the way. Incorporating them in your life can help you as a couple to strive for a long-lasting and meaningful relationship.

Hopefully, you will benefit from these exercises and activities and understand yourself and your partner better. Together, you can instill trust in one another and prevent abuse of trust from the get-go.

In the end, I would like to wish all readers success, happiness, and a budding relationship with their significant other. I would also like to encourage you to have fun and try out the additional set of questions under **Fun Questions for Couple** section, together with your partner. Some questions are fun and casual while others may be thought-provoking and sometimes difficult to answer. But this is where it may help you to build a deeper connection with your partner and it will allow you to navigate and analyze what your relationship lacks, help you fulfill those needs, and establish a trusting relationship.

Fun Questions For Couple

1. If we knew that in five years we would be right where we are now, what things about you and I do today would make me feel the same?

2. If you had a movie made and cast us in the main roles, who would we be playing?

3. What do I need to change for us to continue moving forward as a couple and why would this help us to grow into this role together?

4. If we won $100 million but someone else had to lose $100 million, who would it be and how would we arrange the winnings so there was no loser? (I know its not real money but just go with it)

5. Have you ever cried tears of joy because of me? What made them fall?

6. What's the best I've done for you and how have you expressed your gratitude in return to me?

7. If we were able to go back in time, what would our first date be like and where would it take place at exactly? (don't say a general area, try to get specific)

8. What do I need to do differently so that we can fully commit as one person together on this journey called life. How do I show my appreciation for who you are & so much more?

9. If we were separated for 10 years, how do I know if it was worth the wait for us to join together again as a couple?

10. What makes us better than others? How do we work well together and make each other happy at times when things get tough or hard?

If you like more fun and thought-provoking questions like these, you may look at Connecting Love Question Book for Couple. Please turn to By The Same Author page at the end of this book for more details about this Love Keepsake workbook.

By The Same Author

Connecting Love Question Book For Couple
ISBN: 978-1955847032

LOOKING FOR WAYS TO take your relationship to the next level? Curiosity is a great way to create and sustain intimacy in relationships. ***Connecting Love Question Book for Couple*** has 100 revealing questions that sparks conversations that are fun and meaningful, and at time thought-provoking!

HER

If you had a choice between going on the best date of your life with me or getting $50,000 right now, which would you choose and why?

HIM

HER

Would you rather give up all TV for a year or give up your cell phone for a month? Why?

HIM

AUTHOR NOTE

If you believe that you gained valuable insights from the book and know someone that can seek help from it too, do leave us a humble review on the online bookstores so that it can reach readers who are trying to rebuild trust in their relationships and in their partners. I would love to hear how this helped you deal with the problems in your relationship and any advice that you might have for other couples going through something similar.

Made in United States
North Haven, CT
02 January 2025